COORDINATE GRAPHING-MYSTEI

Table of Contents

Coordinate graphing, or draw by coordinates, math worksheet with:

Pag.

-House 1
-Fishes 3
-Rings stacker toy 5
-Cute young cow 7
-Cute dog 9
-Teapot 11
-Chiken 13
-Cute litlle ghost 15
-Pumpkin 17
-Christmas tree 19
-Snowman 21
-Bucket and shovel for beach 23
-Pinwheel 25
-Mushroom and a snail 27
-Paper airplanes 29
-Flying kite 31
Halloween:
-Witch's shoes 33
-Cat 35
-Apothecary and witch's pot 37
-Bats and tombs 39
-Candies 41
-Witch's hat 43
Christmas:
-Ringing bell 45

Pag.

-Ornaments 47
-Gingerbread 49
-Stockings 51
-Gift boxes 53
-Santa's sack on the slein 55
St. Valentine's Day
-Heart and bow 57
-Number fourteen 59
-Love message 61
-Two friendly hearts 63
-100th day of school learning
  celebration 65
-V is for Valentine 67
-Girls love diamonds 69
St. Patrick's Day
-Trefoil Leaf 71
-Horseshoe and quatrefoil 73
-Leprechaun's top hat 75
-March 17th 77
-Pot-of-gold 79
-Celtic Design 81
Easter holiday themed:
-Two painted eggs 83
-Chocolate bunny 85
-Basket,eggs,bow,chick,sun 87
-Postage stamp painted eggs 89
-Happy Easter! 90

To reveal the mystery picture plot and connect the dots with the given coordinates. Answer included.

Coordinate Graphing / Draw by Coordinates

To reveal the mystery picture plot and connect the dots with coordinates:
(3, 1), (3, 5), (1, 1), (13, 1), (13, 5), (14, 5), (13, 7), (11, 7), (11, 11), (9, 14),
(7, 11), (7, 9), (5, 9), (5, 11), (4, 11), (4, 9), (3, 9), (1, 5), (11, 5), (11, 1)
and
(7, 1), (7, 9), (11, 7), (7, 7), (11, 9), (7, 9).

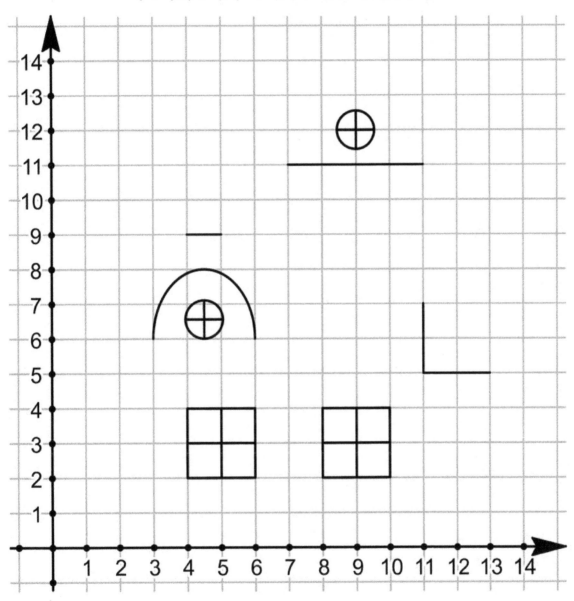

ANSWER:

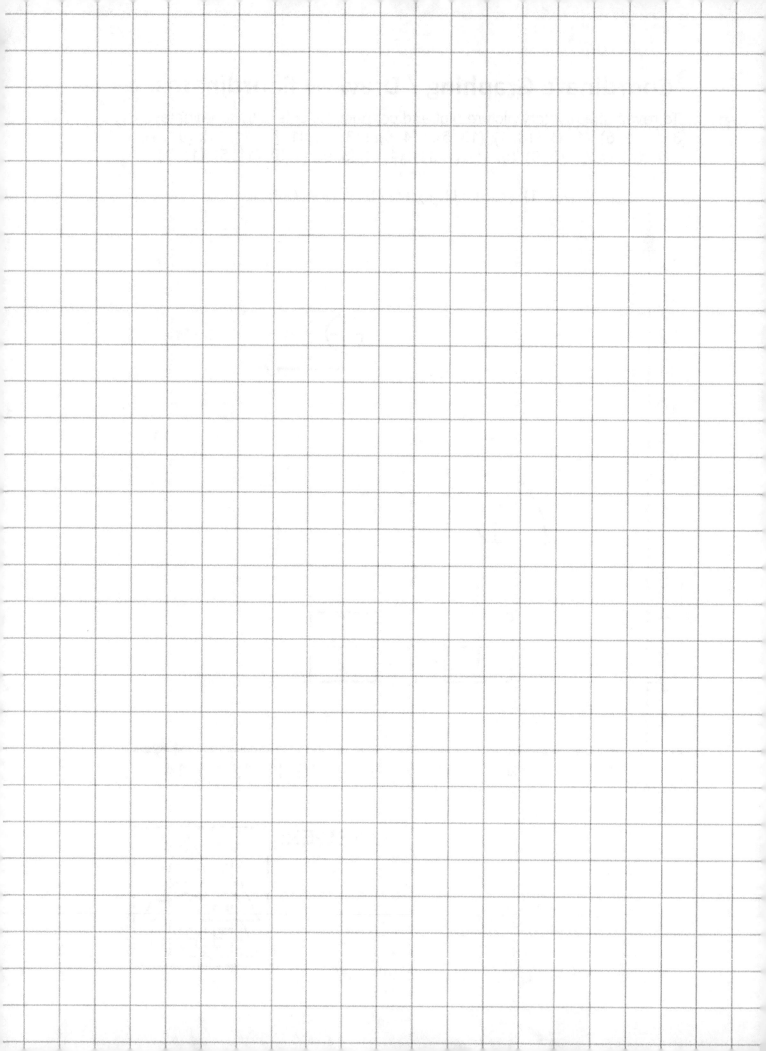

Coordinate Graphing / Draw by Coordinates

To reveal the mystery picture plot and connect the dots with coordinates:
(4, 1), (5, 2), (4, 2), (3, 3), (1, 3), (2, 4), (1, 5), (3, 5), (4, 6), (5, 6), (4, 7), (5, 7),
(6, 6), (7, 6), (9, 4), (7, 2), (6, 2), (5, 1), (4, 1) and (8, 7), (6, 9), (4, 8), (5, 10),
(4, 12), (6, 11), (8, 13), (9, 13), (8, 14), (10, 14), (11, 13), (12, 13), (14, 11),
(14, 9), (12, 7), (11, 7), (10, 6), (8, 6), (9, 7).

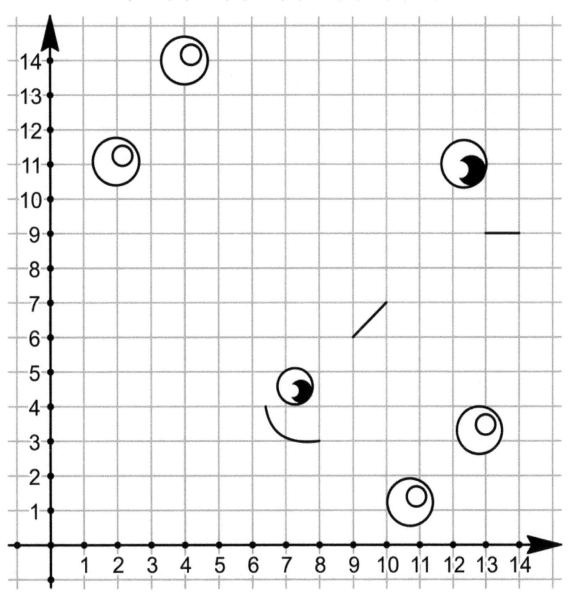

ANSWER:

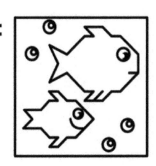

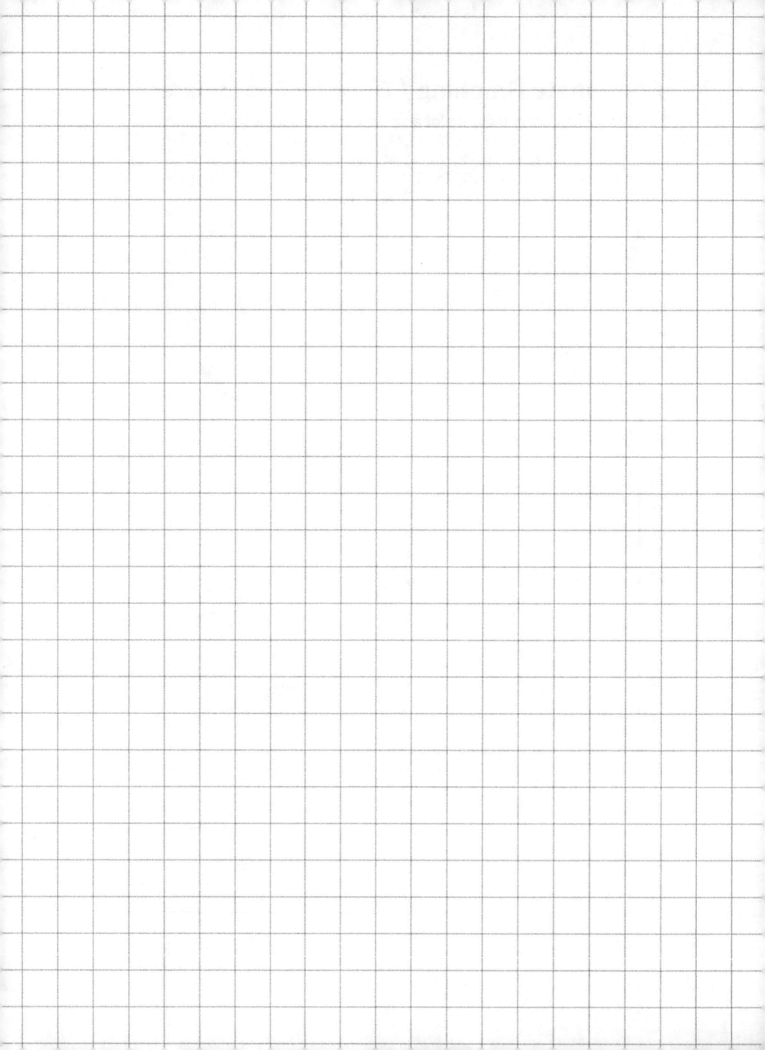

Coordinate Graphing / Draw by Coordinates

To reveal the mystery picture plot and connect the dots with coordinates:
(11, 4), (12, 4), (13, 3), (13, 2), (12, 1), (3, 1), (2, 2), (2, 3), (3, 4), (11, 4), (12, 5), (12, 6), (11, 7), (5, 7), (4, 8), (4, 9), (5, 10), (9, 10), (10, 11), (10, 12), (9, 13), (8, 13), (8, 14), (7, 14), (7, 13), (6, 13), (5, 12), (5, 11), (6, 10).

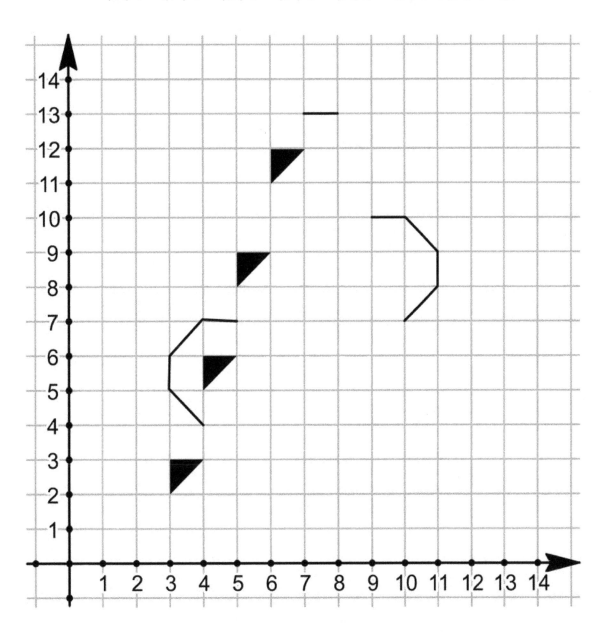

ANSWER:

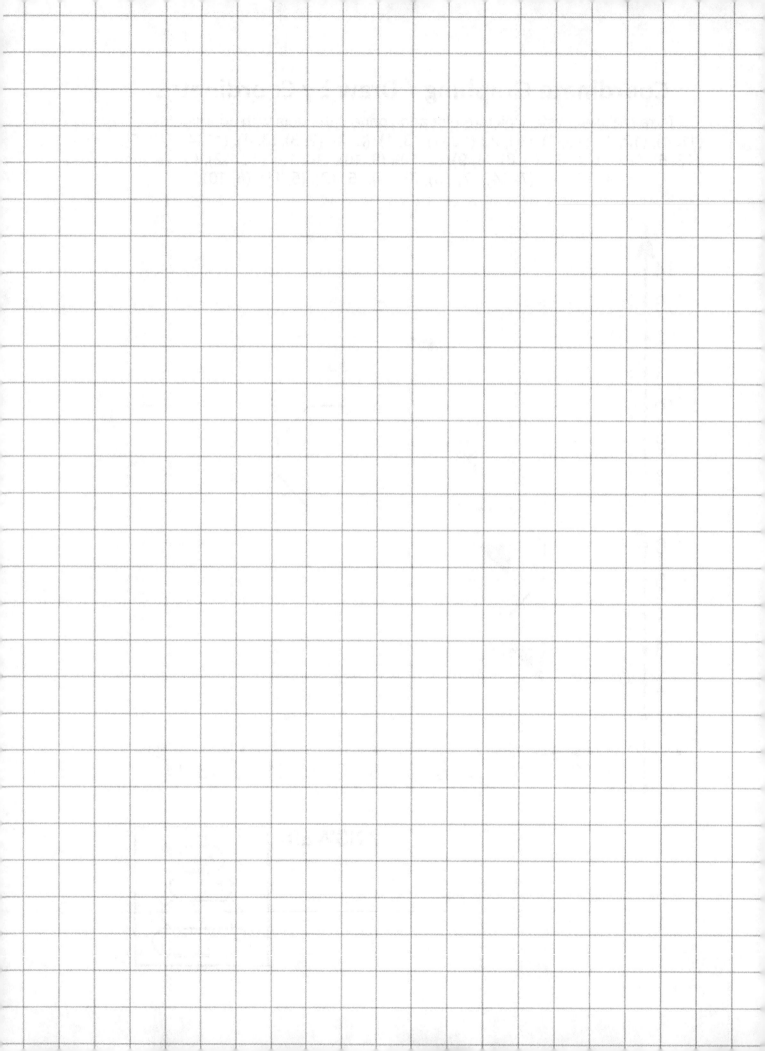

Coordinate Graphing / Draw by Coordinates

To reveal the mystery picture plot and connect the dots with coordinates:
(3, 6), (5, 7), (11, 7), (13, 6), (14, 5), (14, 3), (12, 1), (4, 1), (2, 3), (2, 5), (3, 6), (4, 9), (2, 11), (2, 13), (5, 14), (6, 14), (4, 12), (6, 11), (10, 11), (12, 12), (10, 14), (11, 14), (14, 13), (14, 11), (12, 9), (13, 6) and (3, 4), (5, 3), (11, 3), (13, 4).

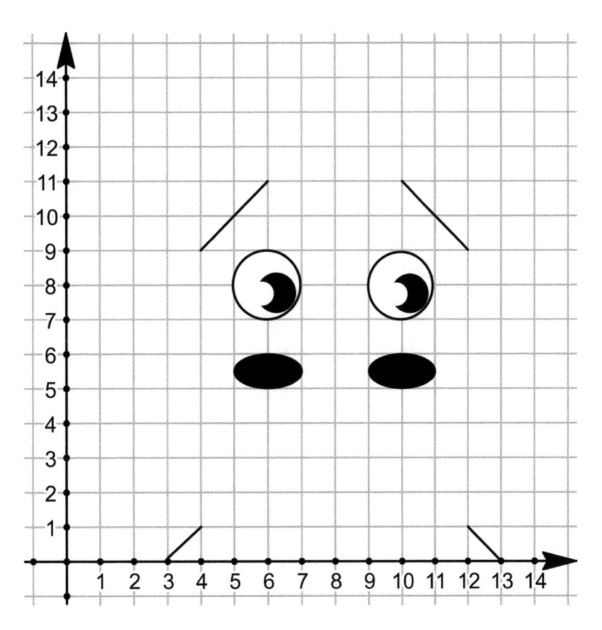

ANSWER:

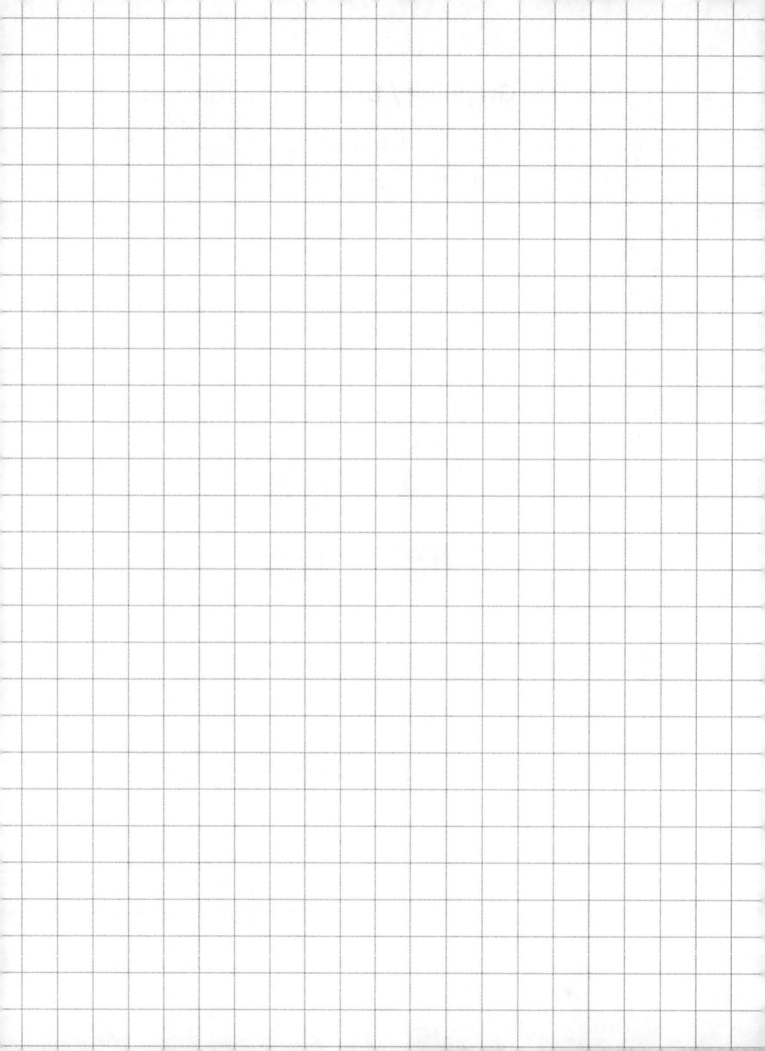

Coordinate Graphing / Draw by Coordinates

To reveal the mystery picture plot and connect the dots with coordinates:
(4, 1), (4, 2), (3, 3), (2, 5), (2, 8), (4, 10), (3, 13), (5, 14), (6, 13), (5, 13), (5, 12), (6, 10), (7, 13), (9, 14), (10, 13), (9, 13), (8, 12), (8, 10), (9, 10), (10, 9), (10, 8), (13, 8), (13, 5), (8, 2), (8, 1), (4, 1).

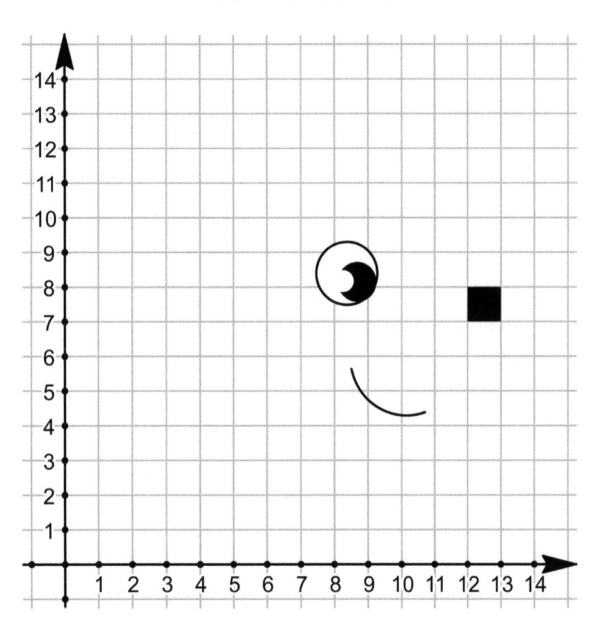

ANSWER:

Coordinate Graphing / Draw by Coordinates

To reveal the mystery picture plot and connect the dots with coordinates:
(10, 11), (9, 10), (11, 9), (12, 6), (12, 9), (13, 10), (13, 9), (14, 9), (13, 8), (14, 5),
(11, 3), (9, 2), (10, 1), (4, 1), (5, 2), (3, 3), (1, 5), (1, 9), (2, 10), (5, 10), (4, 11),
(10, 11), (9, 12), (7, 13), (5, 12), (4, 11)
and (2, 9), (3, 9), (2, 6), (2, 9).

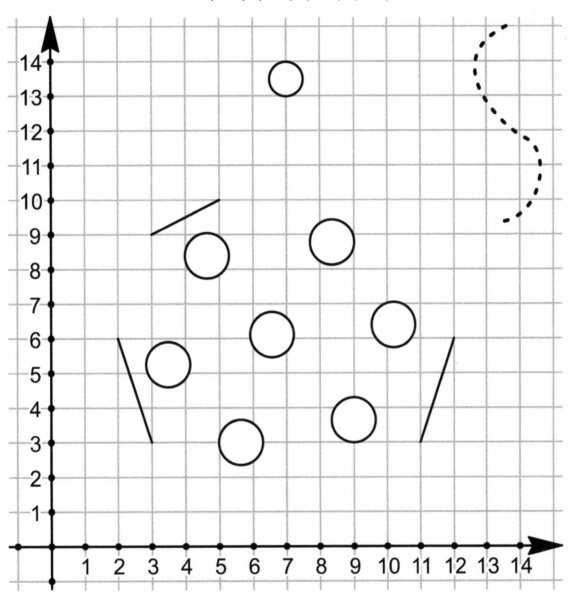

ANSWER:

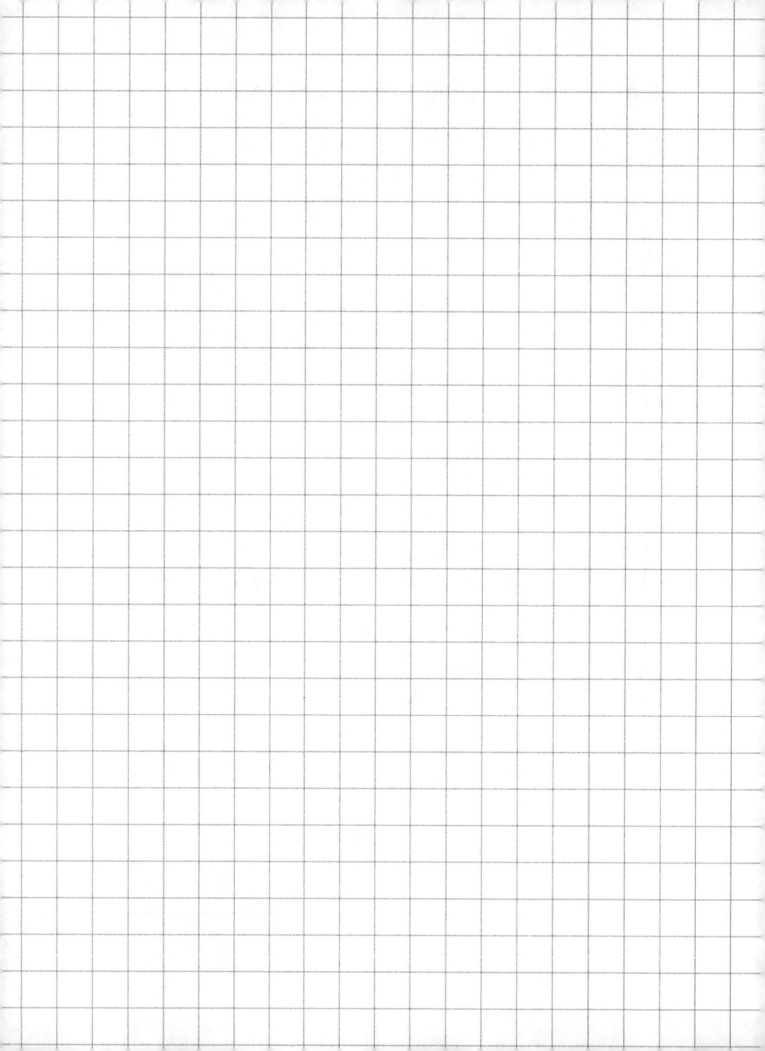

Coordinate Graphing / Draw by Coordinates

To reveal the mystery picture plot and connect the dots with coordinates:
(11, 13), (12, 12), (13, 12), (12, 11), (13, 10), (12, 10), (12, 6), (11, 4), (9, 3),
(10, 2), (12, 1), (9, 1), (9, 2), (8, 3), (7, 3), (6, 2), (8, 1), (5, 1), (5, 2), (6, 3), (3, 5),
(2, 7), (2, 10), (4, 9), (7, 9), (8, 10), (8, 12), (9, 13), (11, 13), (11, 14), (10, 13),
(9, 14), (9, 13) and (4, 8), (5, 6), (8, 5), (9, 7).

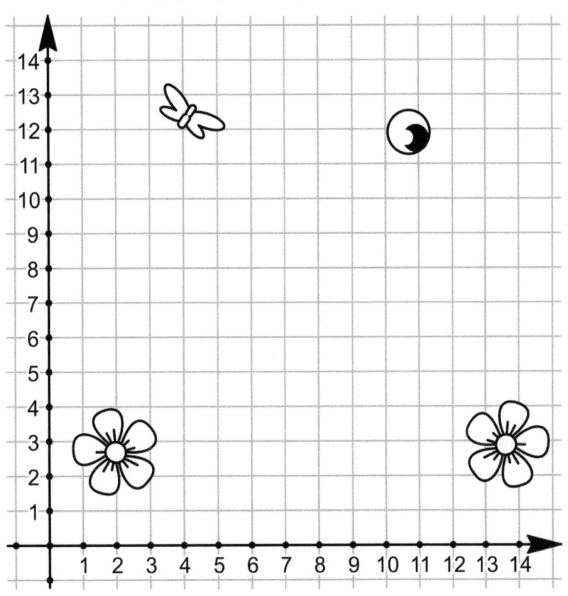

ANSWER:

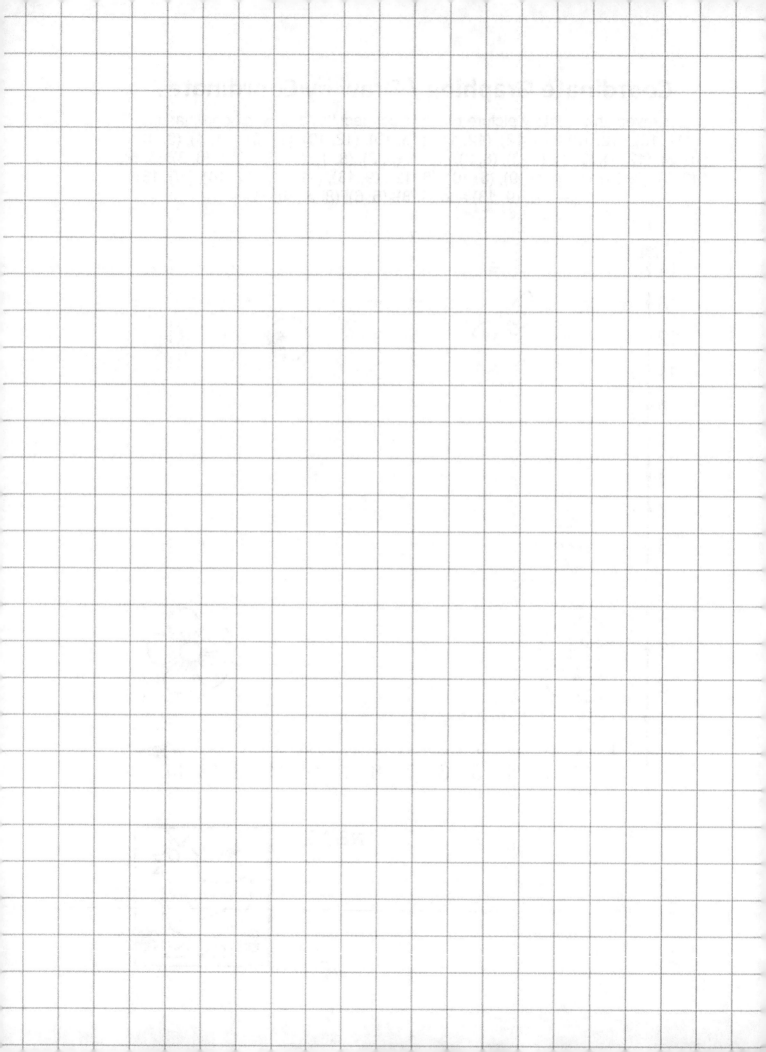

Coordinate Graphing / Draw by Coordinates

To reveal the mystery picture plot and connect the dots with coordinates:
(6, 10), (7, 12), (8, 13), (10, 13), (11, 12), (12, 10), (12, 9), (13, 9), (14, 8),
(11, 6), (9, 3), (6, 1), (4, 1), (4, 3), (3, 4), (3, 6), (2, 7), (2, 8), (1, 10), (4, 10),
(5, 8), (6, 7), (7, 8), (7, 9), (5, 11), (4, 11), (4, 10).

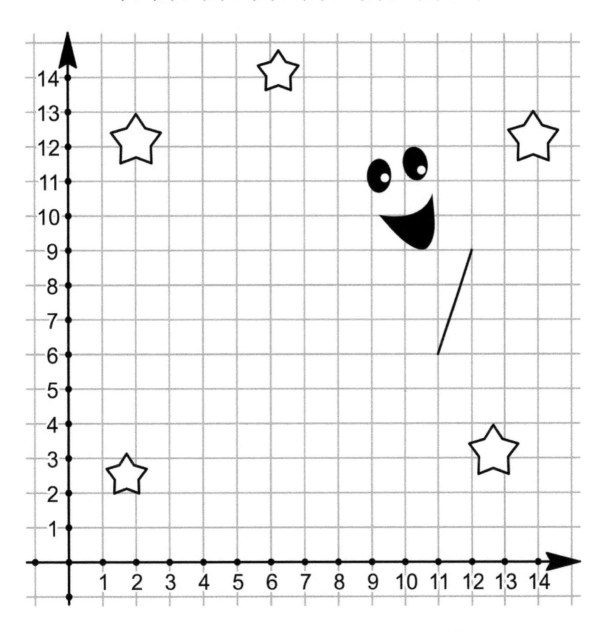

ANSWER:

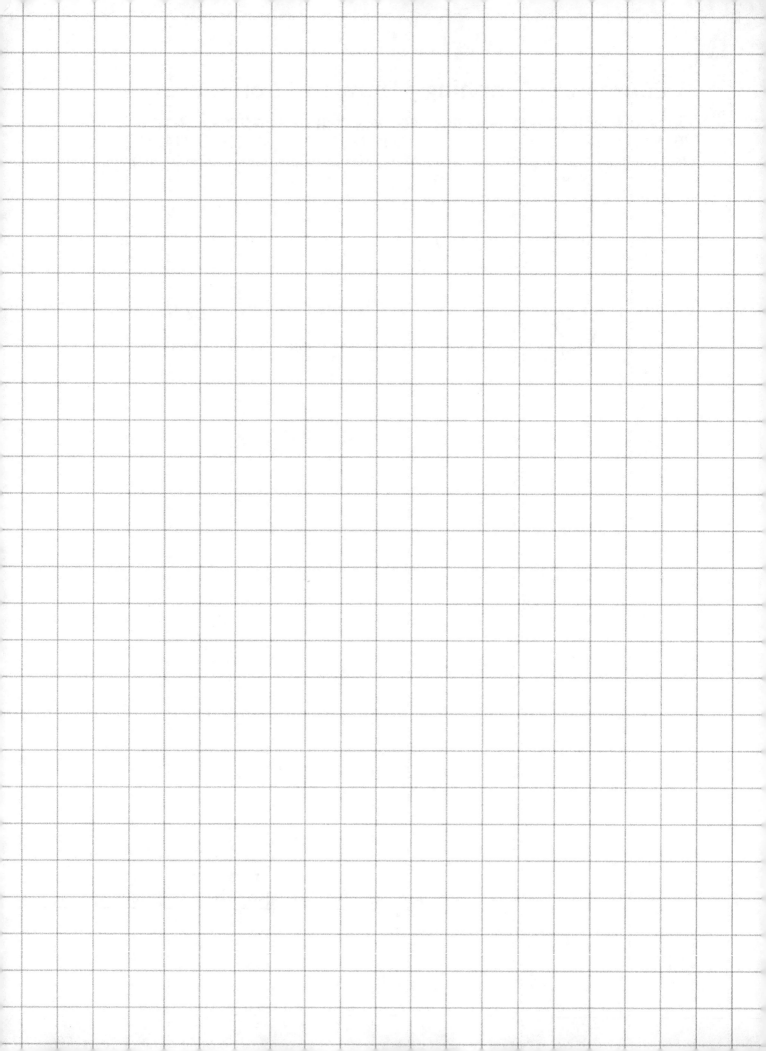

Coordinate Graphing / Draw by Coordinates

To reveal the mystery picture plot and connect the dots with coordinates:
(9, 11), (11, 11), (13, 10), (14, 8), (14, 4), (13, 2), (11, 1), (4, 1), (2, 2), (1, 4), (1, 8),
(2, 10), (4, 11), (6, 11), (7, 12), (8, 14), (9, 14), (11, 13), (10, 12), (9, 13), (8, 12),
(9, 11), (8, 10), (6, 11) and (2, 6), (4, 5), (7, 5), (7, 4), (8, 4), (8, 5), (11, 5), (13, 6),
(10, 3), (10, 4), (9, 4), (9, 3), (6, 3), (6, 4), (5, 4), (5, 3), (2, 6) and (3, 9), (5, 8), (5, 7),
(4, 7), (3, 9) and (10, 8), (10, 7), (11, 7), (12, 9), (10, 8).

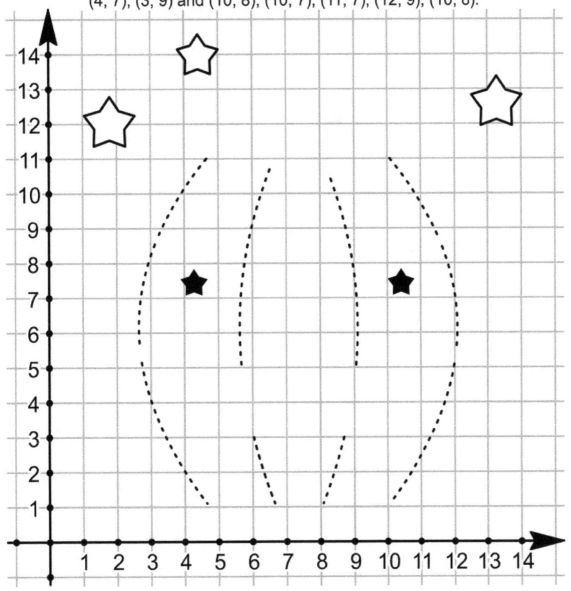

ANSWER:

Coordinate Graphing / Draw by Coordinates

To reveal the mystery picture plot and connect the dots with coordinates:
(3, 5), (4, 5), (2, 2), (6, 2), (6, 1), (8, 1), (8, 2), (12, 2), (10, 5), (11, 5), (9, 8), (10, 8), (8, 11), (9, 11), (7, 14), (5, 11), (6, 11), (4, 8), (5, 8), (3, 5).

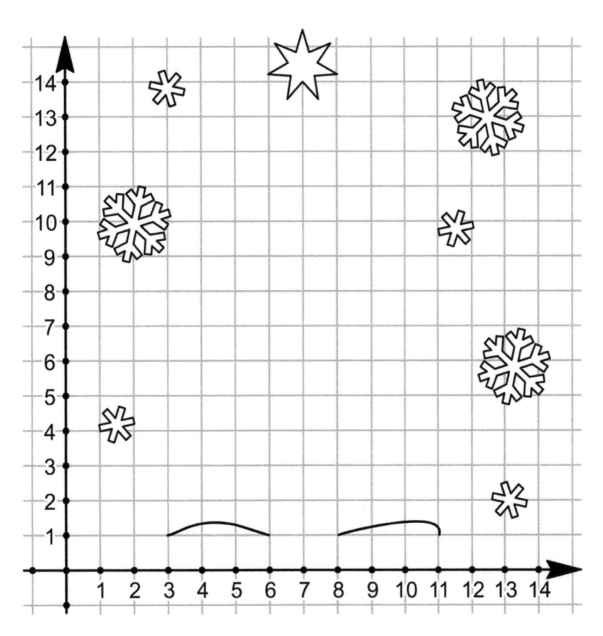

ANSWER:

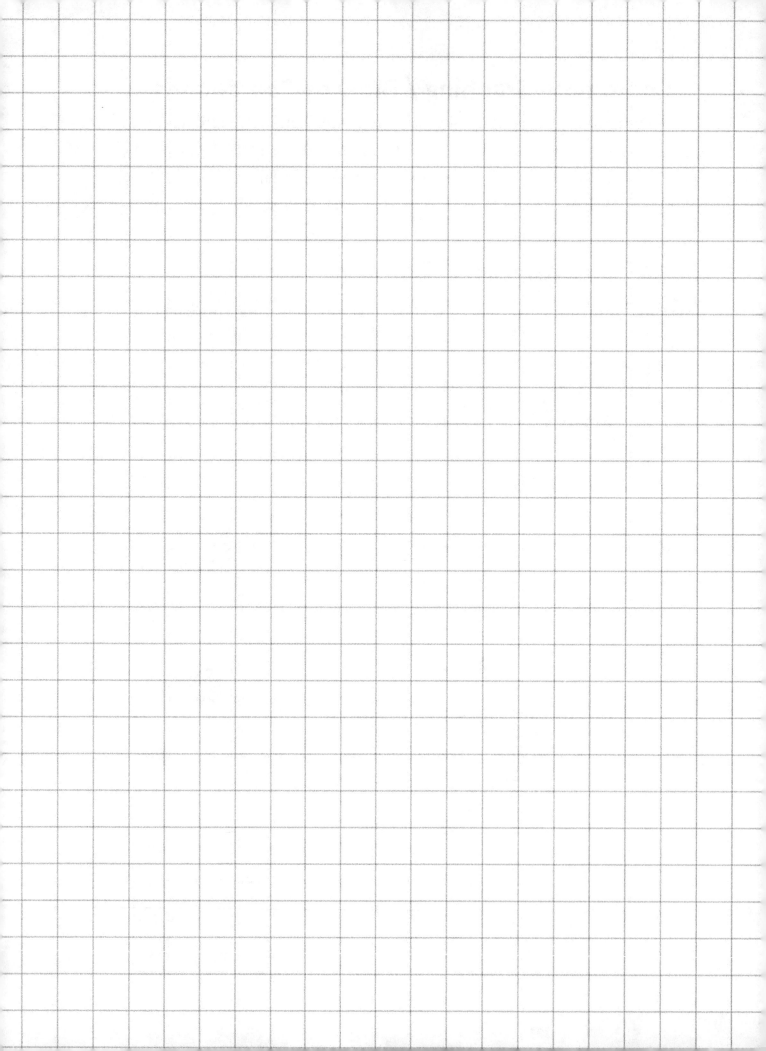

Coordinate Graphing / Draw by Coordinates

To reveal the mystery picture plot and connect the dots with coordinates:

(6, 12), (9, 11), (9, 9), (8, 8), (10, 7), (11, 8), (12, 7), (11, 5), (11, 3), (10, 1), (4, 1),
(3, 3), (3, 5), (2, 6), (2, 7), (4, 7), (6, 8), (5, 9), (5, 11), (7, 13), (6, 14), (8, 14), (9, 11).

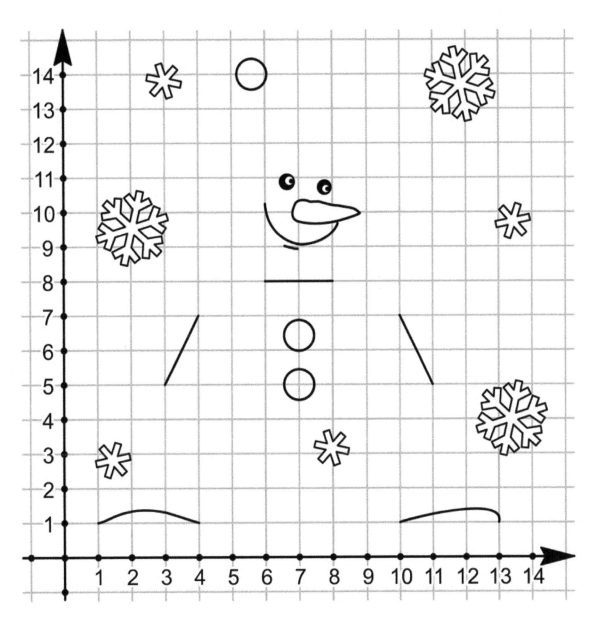

ANSWER:

Coordinate Graphing / Draw by Coordinates

To reveal the mystery picture plot and connect the dots with coordinates:
(10, 2), (9, 1), (7, 1), (5, 3), (5, 5), (4, 6), (2, 6), (3, 7), (4, 7), (6, 5), (6, 4), (8, 2),
(12, 2), (14, 10), (11, 14), (7, 14), (4, 10), (13, 10), (11, 13), (7, 13), (5, 10)
and (1, 3), (4, 3), (4, 1), (1, 1), (1, 3).

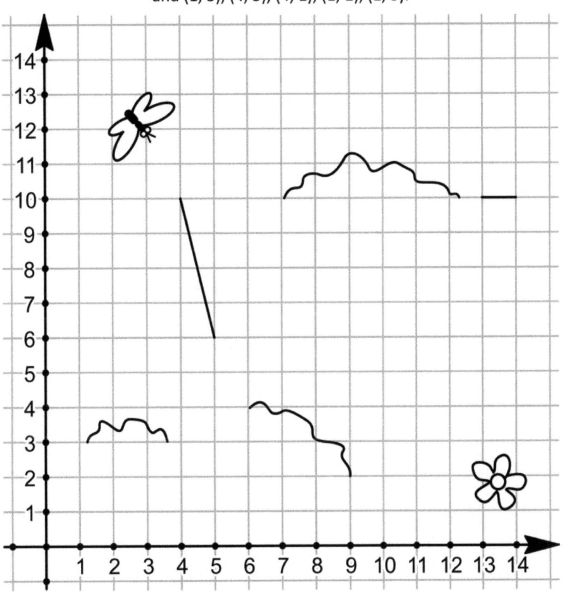

ANSWER:

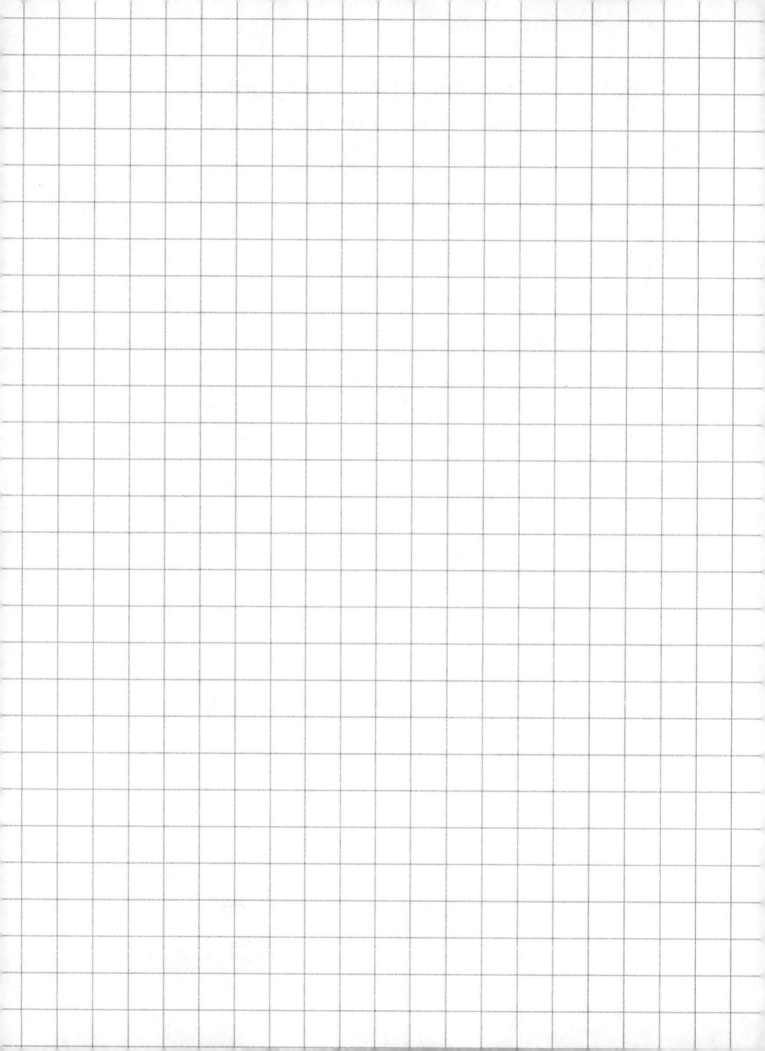

Coordinate Graphing / Draw by Coordinates

To reveal the mystery picture plot and connect the dots with coordinates:
(3, 12), (13, 2), (13, 7), (8, 7), (8, 12), (13, 12), (3, 2), (8, 2), (8, 7),
(3, 7), (3, 12).

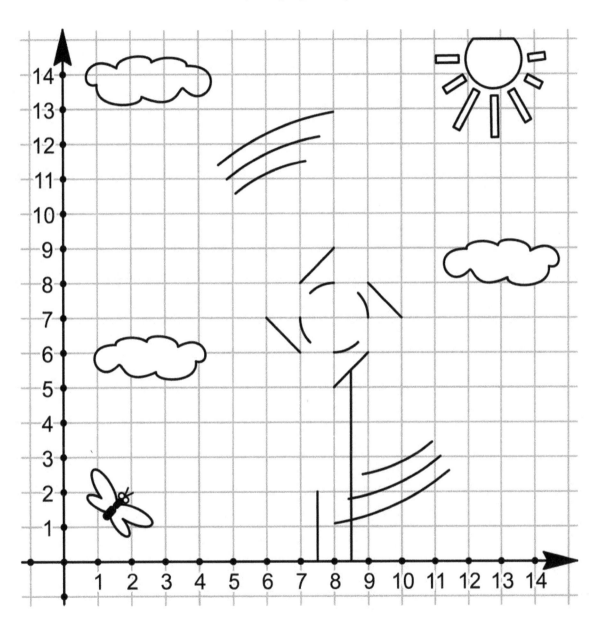

ANSWER:

Coordinate Graphing / Draw by Coordinates

To reveal the mystery picture plot and connect the dots with coordinates:

(4, 8), (1, 8), (1, 9), (2, 12), (4, 13), (8, 13), (10, 12), (11, 9), (11, 8), (4, 8), (3, 3), (3, 2), (4, 1), (8, 1), (9, 2), (9, 3), (8, 8).

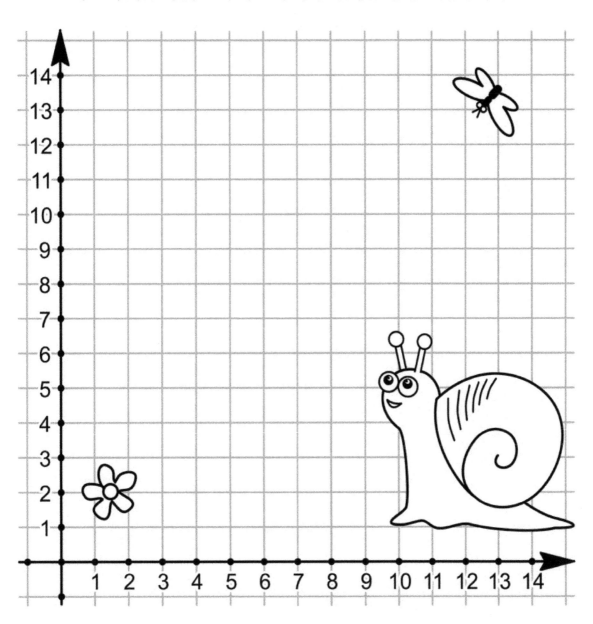

ANSWER:

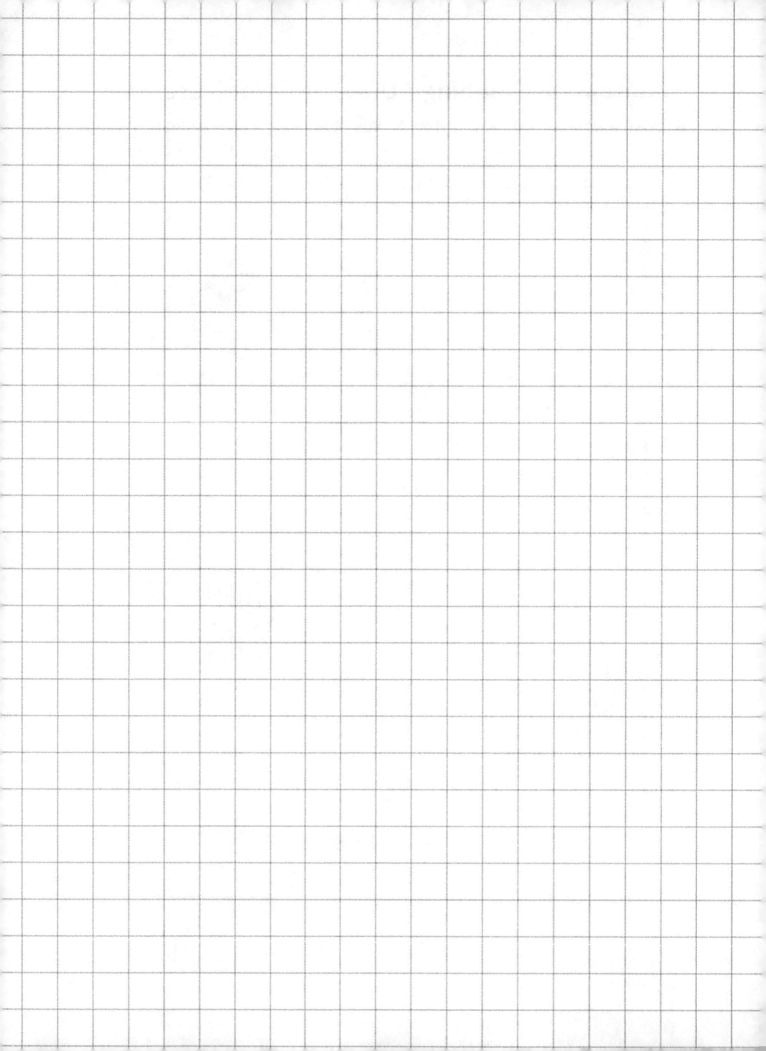

Coordinate Graphing / Draw by Coordinates

To reveal the mystery picture plot and connect the dots with coordinates:
(10, 13), (2, 11), (3, 8), (3, 10), (6, 8), (10, 13), (3, 10)
and (6, 5), (14, 7), (5, 6), (6, 5), (7, 2), (7, 4), (14, 7), (10, 2), (7, 4).

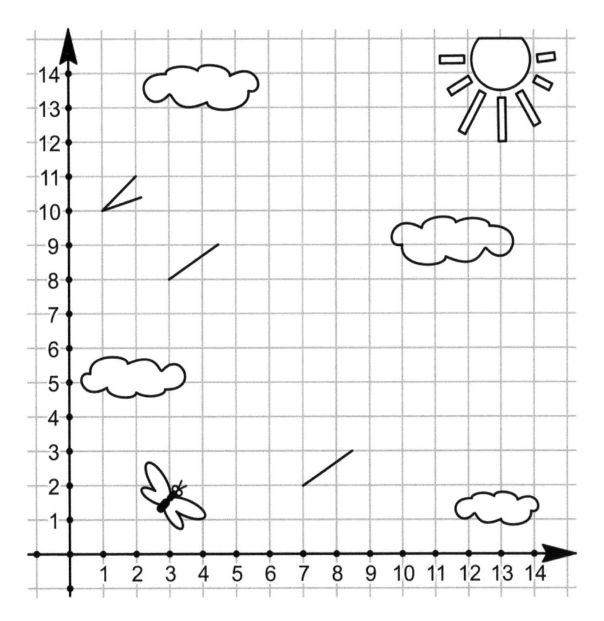

ANSWER:

Coordinate Graphing / Draw by Coordinates

To reveal the mystery picture plot and connect the dots with coordinates:

(2, 1), (3, 3), (5, 4), (6, 6), (8, 7), (13, 10), (12, 14), (8, 13), (8, 7),

(12, 14).

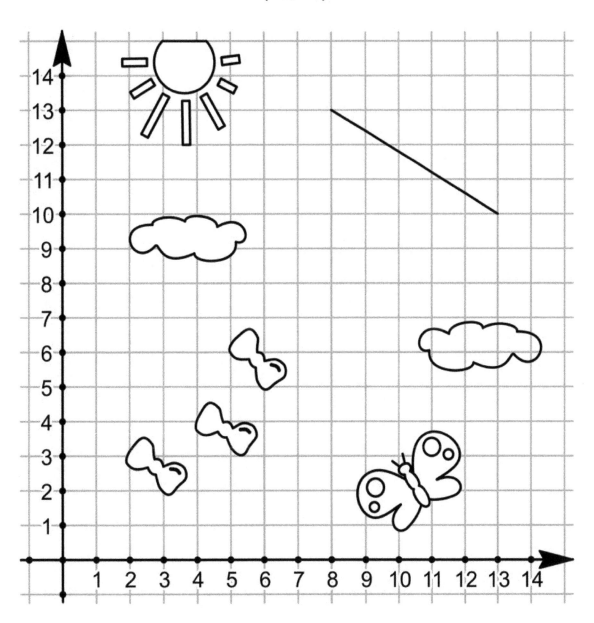

ANSWER:

Coordinate Graphing / Draw by Coordinates

To reveal the mystery picture plot and connect the dots with coordinates:
(4, 11), (8, 8), (9, 8), (9, 10), (11, 8), (12, 8), (14, 9), (13, 7), (10, 6), (8, 6), (7, 7),
(5, 8), (5, 6), (4, 6), (3, 8), (3, 10), (4, 11) and (12, 4), (11, 2), (8, 1), (6, 1), (5, 2),
(3, 3), (3, 1), (2, 1), (1, 3), (1, 5), (2, 6), (6, 3), (7, 3), (7, 5), (9, 3), (10, 3), (12, 4).

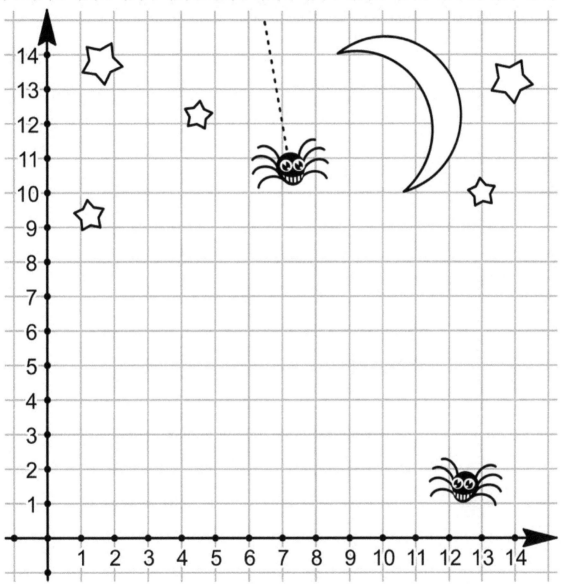

ANSWER:

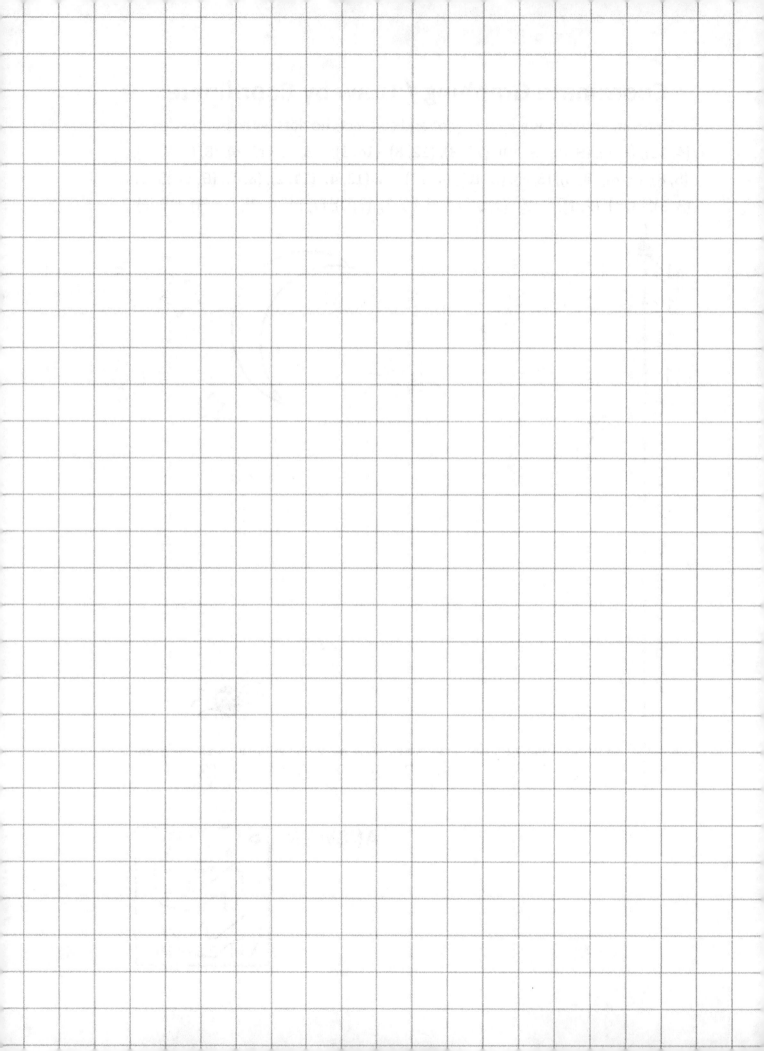

Coordinate Graphing / Draw by Coordinates

To reveal the mystery picture plot and connect the dots with coordinates:
(5, 9), (7, 9), (6, 12), (7, 14), (10, 14), (12, 13), (13, 12), (13, 11), (12, 11), (10, 12), (8, 12),
(9, 9), (8, 8), (6, 8), (4, 10), (4, 9), (3, 8), (2, 5), (4, 2), (4, 1), (6, 1), (7, 2), (9, 2), (9, 1),
(11, 1), (12, 2), (14, 5), (13, 8), (11, 9), (10, 9), (10, 8), (11, 6), (10, 4), (8, 3), (6, 3), (4, 4),
(3, 6), (4, 8), (4, 9) and (5, 5), (6, 4), (8, 4), (9, 5).

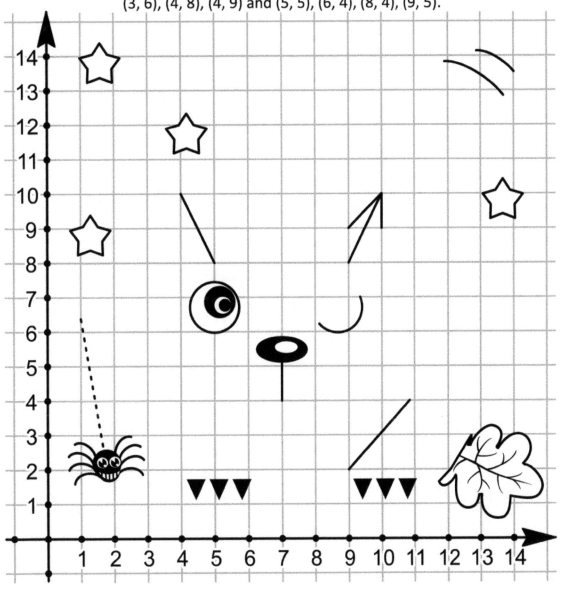

ANSWER:

Coordinate Graphing / Draw by Coordinates

To reveal the mystery picture plot and connect the dots with coordinates:
(1, 10), (3, 10), (2, 11), (2, 12), (3, 13), (3, 14), (4, 14), (4, 13), (5, 12), (5, 11), (4, 10),
(7, 10), (6, 11), (6, 13), (7, 13), (7, 14), (8, 14), (8, 13), (9, 13), (9, 11), (8, 10), (10, 10),
(11, 13), (11, 14), (12, 14), (12, 13), (13, 10), (14, 10) and (5, 2), (4, 1), (6, 1), (6, 2),
(9, 2), (9, 1), (11, 1), (10, 2), (11, 3), (12, 6), (11, 8), (4, 8), (3, 6), (4, 3), (5, 2).

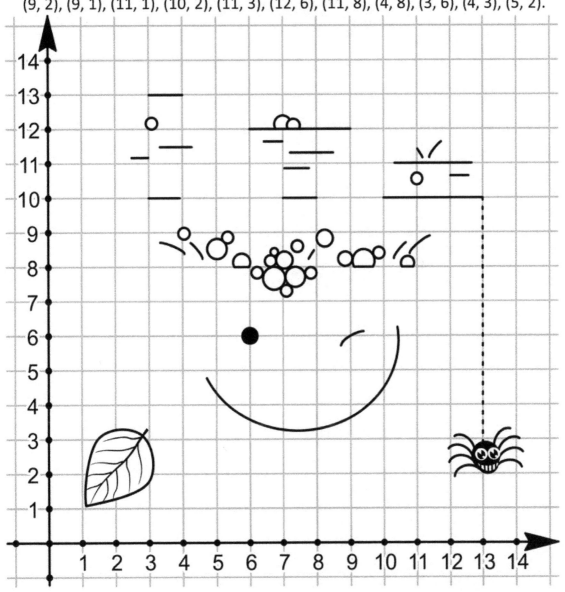

ANSWER:

Coordinate Graphing / Draw by Coordinates

To reveal the mystery picture plot and connect the dots with coordinates:
(3, 11), (2, 11), (2, 12), (3, 12), (3, 13), (4, 13), (4, 12), (5, 13), (8, 14), (7, 12), (6, 12), (6, 11), (5, 11), (6, 10), (6, 9), (5, 9), (4, 10), (4, 9), (3, 9), (3, 8), (1, 7), (2, 10), (3, 11) and (12, 10), (12, 9), (13, 9), (13, 8), (12, 8), (13, 7), (14, 4), (12, 5), (12, 6), (11, 6), (11, 7), (10, 6), (9, 6), (9, 7), (10, 8), (9, 8), (9, 9), (8, 9), (7, 11), (10, 10), (11, 9), (11, 10), (12, 10) and (1, 1), (2, 1), (2, 5), (3, 6), (5, 6), (6, 5), (6, 1), (7, 1), (7, 4), (8, 5), (10, 5), (11, 4), (11, 1), (14, 1).

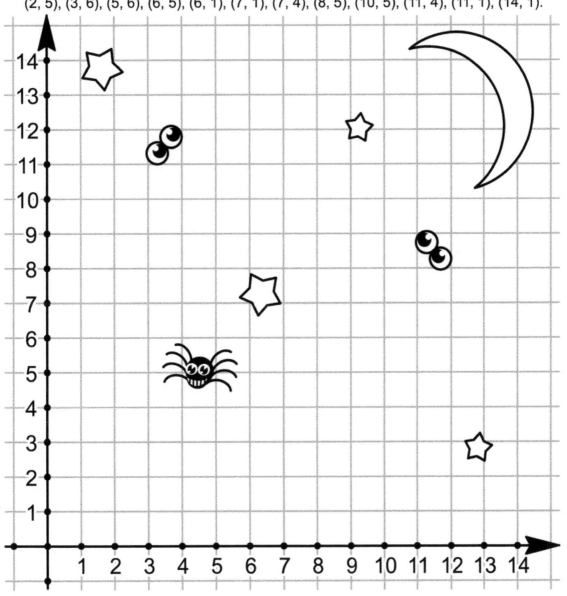

ANSWER:

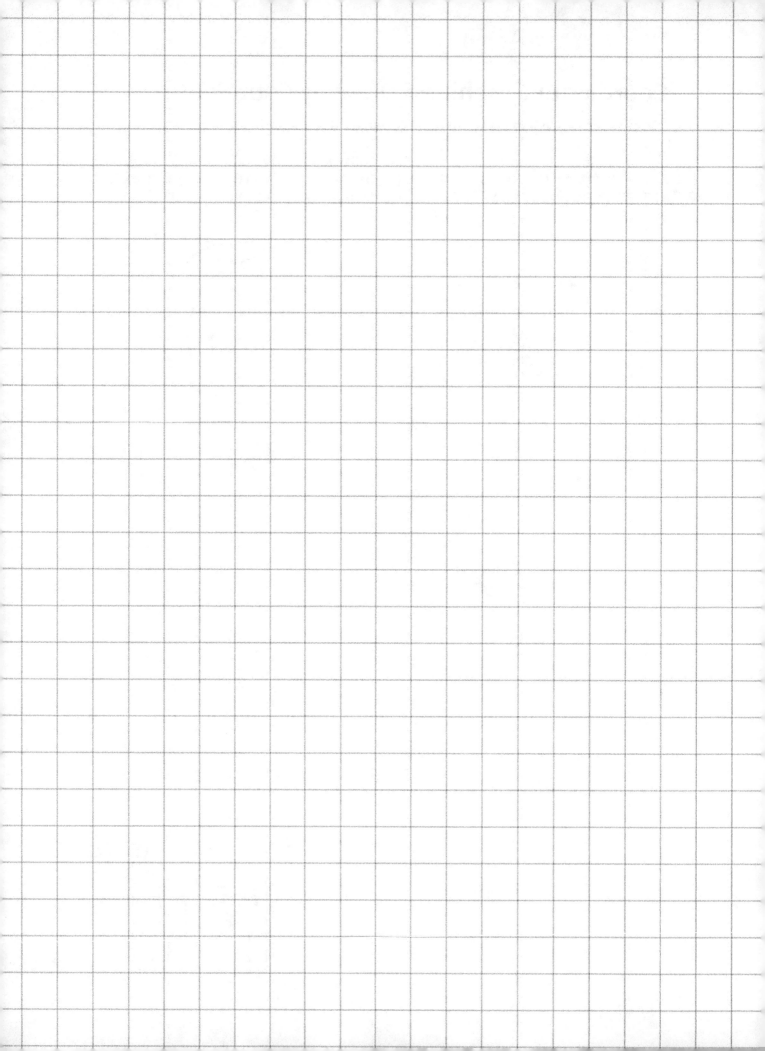

Coordinate Graphing / Draw by Coordinates

To reveal the mystery picture plot and connect the dots with coordinates:
(5, 11), (5, 10), (4, 9), (2, 9), (1, 10), (1, 11), (2, 13), (4, 13), (5, 11), (1, 11) and (9, 12), (10, 13),
(11, 13), (11, 12), (12, 12), (12, 11), (13, 11), (13, 10), (12, 9), (10, 9), (10, 7), (9, 5), (7, 4),
(5, 4), (5, 2), (4, 1), (3, 1), (3, 2), (2, 2), (2, 3), (1, 3), (1, 4), (2, 5), (4, 5), (4, 7), (5, 9), (7, 10),
(9, 10), (9, 12 and (10, 3), (10, 2), (11, 1), (13, 1), (14, 2), (14, 3), (10, 3), (11, 5), (13, 5), (14, 3).

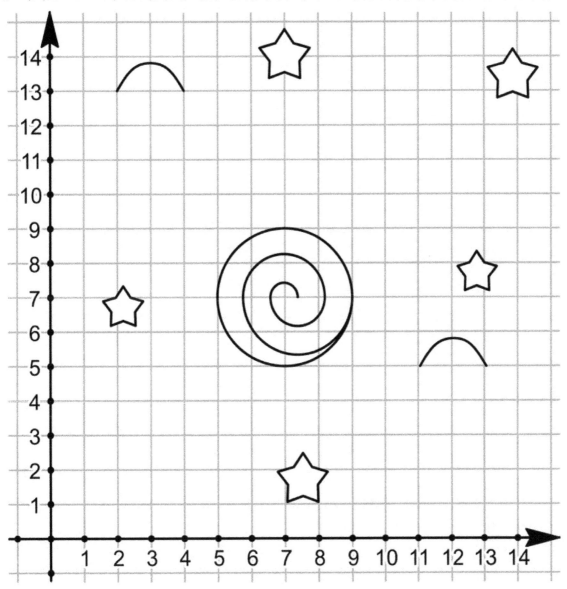

ANSWER:

Coordinate Graphing / Draw by Coordinates

To reveal the mystery picture plot and connect the dots with coordinates:
(12, 9), (11, 10), (9, 11), (9, 10), (10, 7), (11, 5), (12, 4), (13, 4), (14, 3), (13, 2),
(9, 1), (6, 1), (2, 2), (1, 3), (2, 4), (3, 4), (4, 5), (6, 11), (8, 14), (9, 14), (11, 11),
(12, 9).

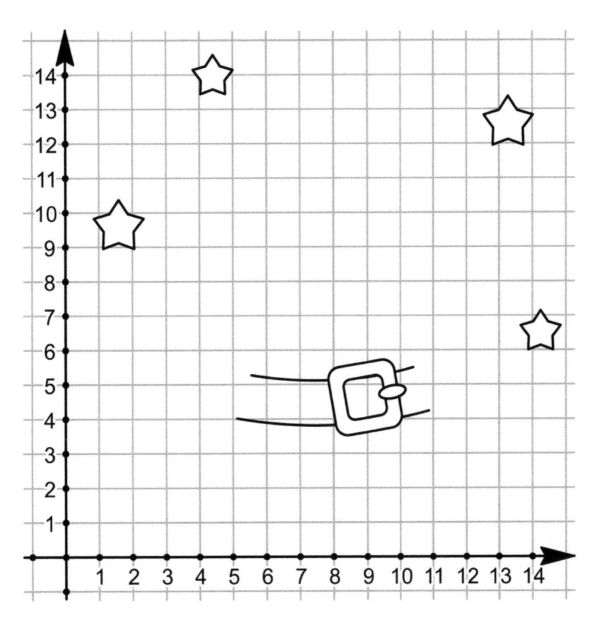

ANSWER:

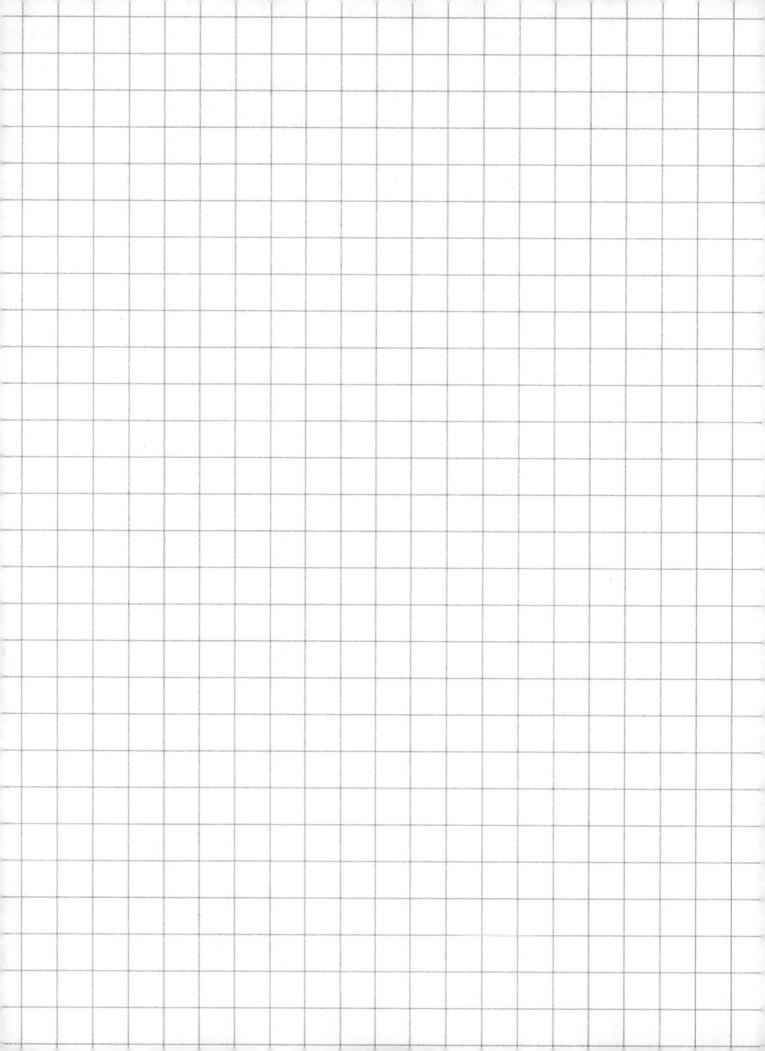

Coordinate Graphing / Draw by Coordinates

To reveal the mystery picture plot and connect the dots with coordinates:

(2, 10), (4, 7), (7, 10), (7, 11), (4, 13), (3, 11), (3, 10), (4, 8), (7, 10), (8, 10), (8, 11), (11, 13), (12, 11), (12, 10), (11, 8), (8, 10), (11, 7), (13, 10) and (6, 9), (5, 7), (4, 4), (3, 4), (3, 2), (12, 2), (12, 4), (11, 4), (10, 7), (9, 9) and (8, 14), (8, 11), (7, 11), (7, 14).

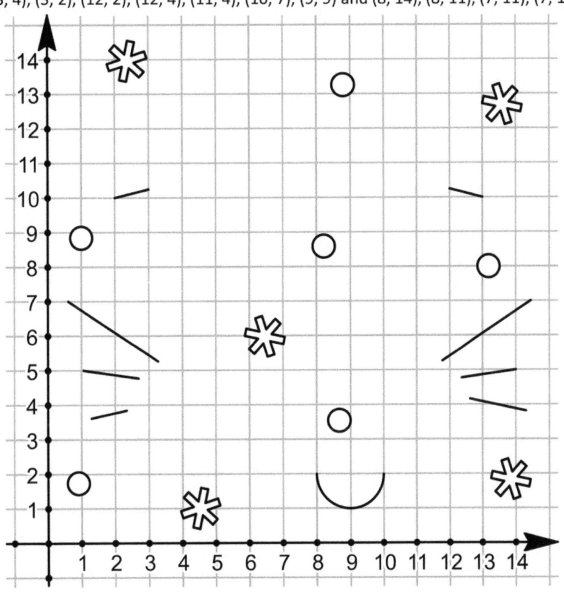

ANSWER:

Coordinate Graphing / Draw by Coordinates

To reveal the mystery picture plot and connect the dots with coordinates:
(9, 10), (9, 11), (11, 11), (11, 10), (9, 10), (7, 9), (6, 7), (6, 5), (7, 3),
(9, 2), (11, 2), (13, 3), (14, 5), (14, 7), (13, 9), (11, 10) and (6, 3), (4, 3),
(2, 4), (1, 6), (1, 8), (2, 10), (4, 11), (4, 12), (6, 12), (6,11), (8, 10).

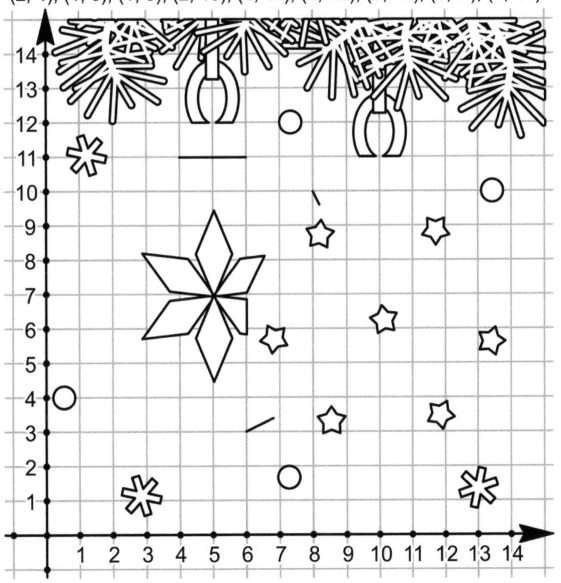

ANSWER:

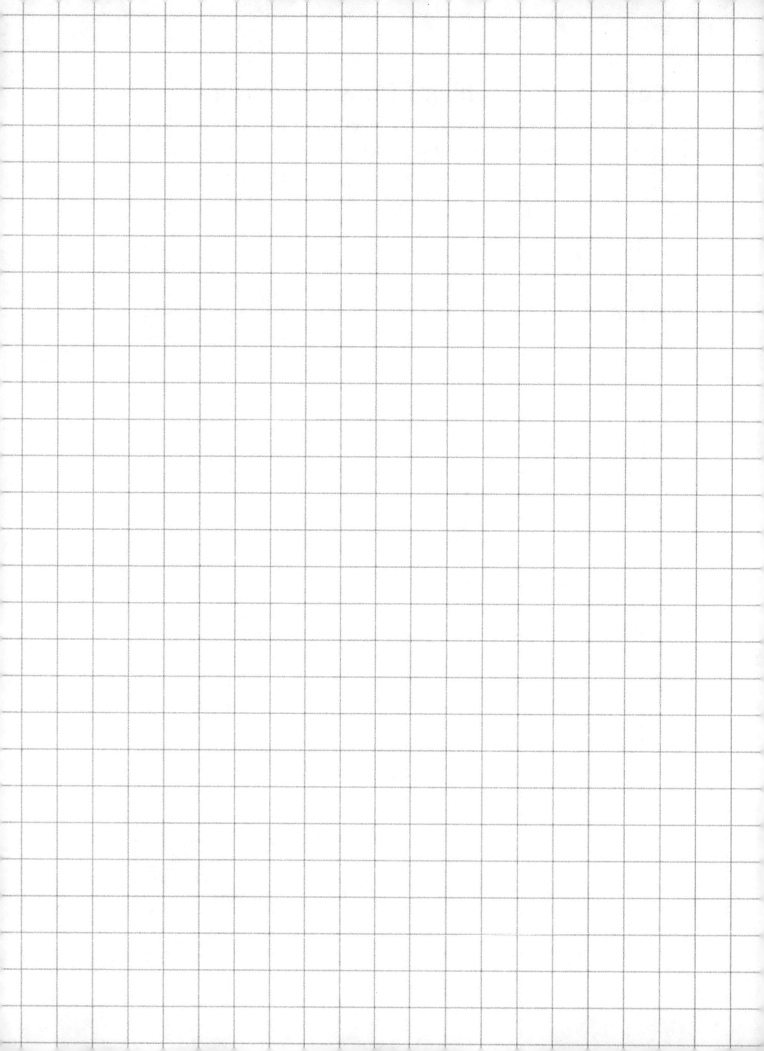

Coordinate Graphing / Draw by Coordinates

To reveal the mystery picture plot and connect the dots with coordinates:

(10, 7), (10, 5), (11, 3), (12, 2), (11, 1), (10, 1), (9, 2), (8, 4), (7, 2), (6, 1), (5, 1), (4, 2), (5, 3), (6, 5), (6, 7), (4, 6), (3, 7), (4, 8), (6, 9), (7, 9), (6, 10), (6, 12), (7, 13), (9, 13), (10, 12), (10, 10), (9, 9), (10, 9), (12, 8), (13, 7), (12, 6), (10, 7).

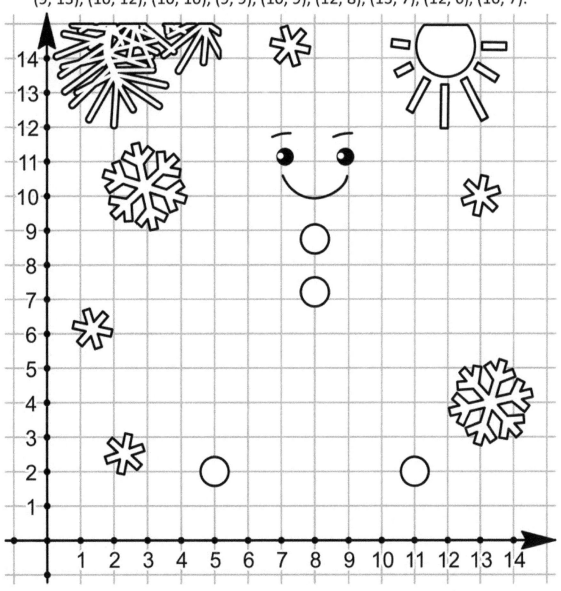

ANSWER:

Coordinate Graphing / Draw by Coordinates

To reveal the mystery picture plot and connect the dots with coordinates:
(2, 2), (2, 3), (3, 10), (6, 9), (5, 4), (7, 2), (7, 1), (6, 1), (3, 2), (2, 2)
and (9, 10), (12, 9), (11, 4), (13, 2), (13, 1), (12, 1), (9, 2), (8, 2),
(8, 3), (9, 10).

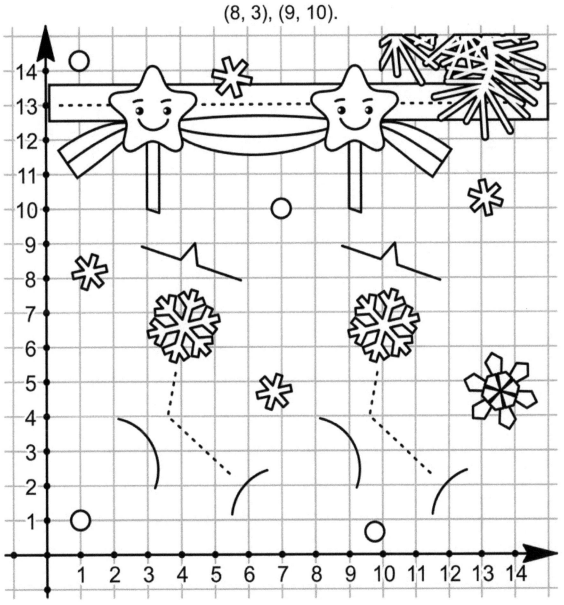

ANSWER:

Coordinate Graphing / Draw by Coordinates

To reveal the mystery picture plot and connect the dots with coordinates:
(3, 5), (1, 5), (1, 3), (2, 3), (2, 1), (8, 1), (8, 2), (13, 2), (13, 7), (14, 7), (14, 9), (7, 9), (7, 7), (8, 7), (8, 5), (3, 5), (3, 10), (2, 10), (2, 12), (10, 12), (10, 10), (3, 10).

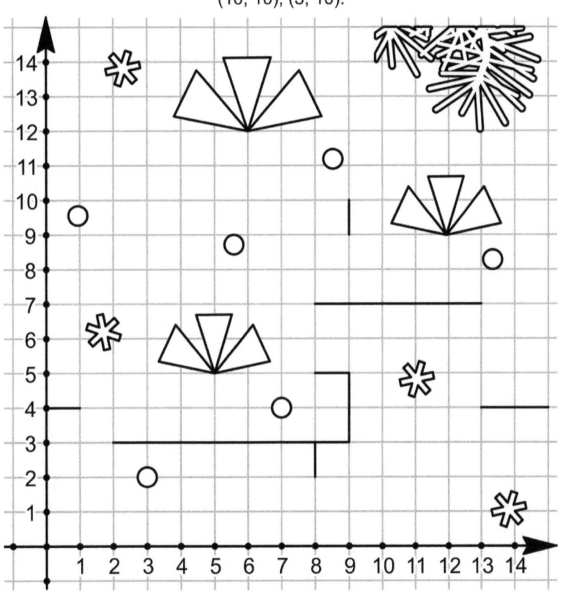

ANSWER:

Coordinate Graphing / Draw by Coordinates

To reveal the mystery picture plot and connect the dots with coordinates:
(1, 12), (1, 8), (2, 5), (1, 5), (1, 4), (2, 4), (2, 2), (1, 2), (1, 1), (12, 1),
(14, 3), (14, 6), (13, 6), (13, 3), (12, 2), (11, 2), (11, 4), (12, 4), (12, 5),
(8, 5), (6, 9), (2, 12), (1, 12).

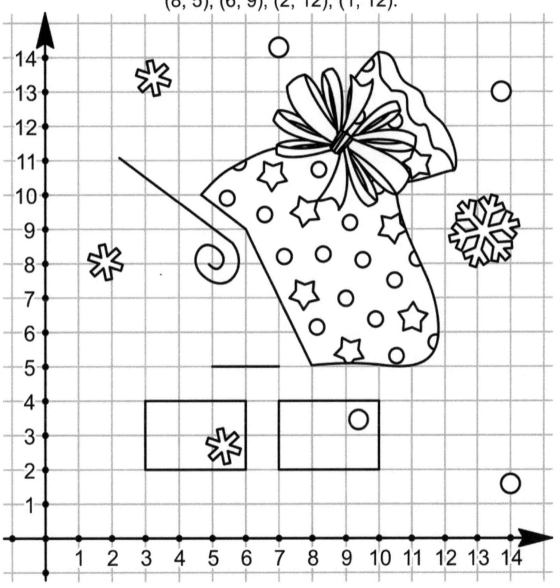

ANSWER:

Coordinate Graphing / Draw by Coordinates

To reveal the mystery picture plot and connect the dots with coordinates:
(14, 6), (12, 3), (9, 6), (12, 4), (13, 6), (13, 7), (12, 9), (9, 7), (3, 12), (5, 12),
(7, 11), (9, 12), (11, 12), (12, 11), (13, 9), (13, 7) and (9, 7), (9, 6), (8, 6),
(8, 7), (5, 9), (4, 7), (4, 6), (5, 4), (8, 6), (5, 3), (3, 6) and (4, 7), (1, 9), (1, 7),
(3, 4), (7, 1), (11, 4).

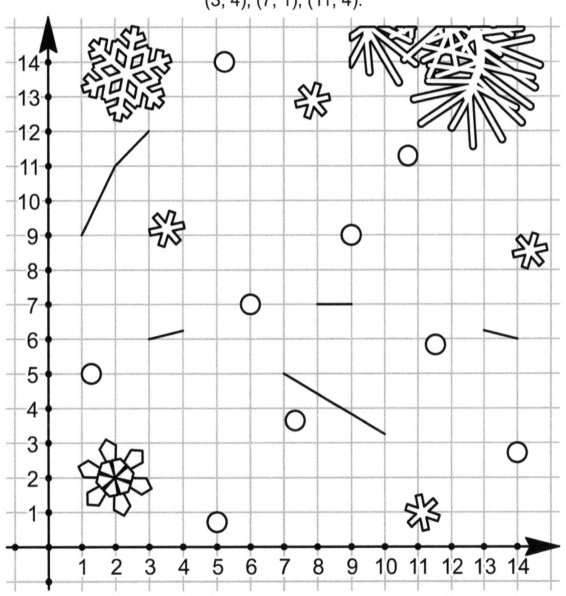

ANSWER:

Coordinate Graphing / Draw by Coordinates

To reveal the mystery picture plot and connect the dots with coordinates:
(1, 10), (1, 9), (3, 10), (3, 1), (6, 1), (6, 13), (4, 13), (1, 10)
and (7, 6), (7, 4), (11, 4), (11, 1), (14, 1), (14, 13), (12, 13), (7, 6)
and (9, 6), (11, 9), (11, 6), (9, 6).

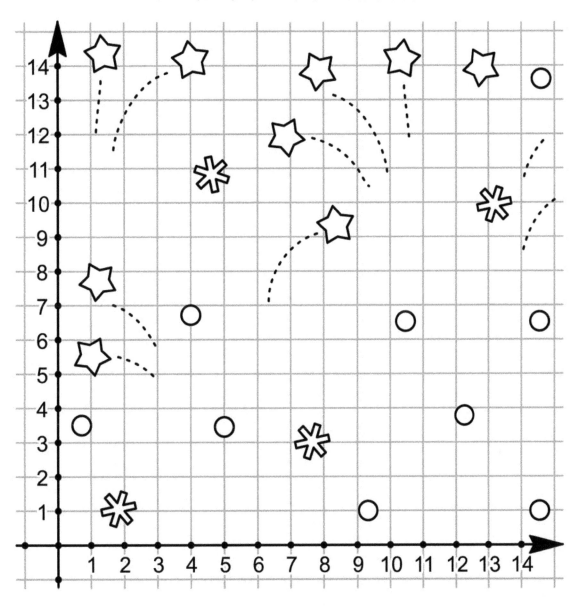

ANSWER:

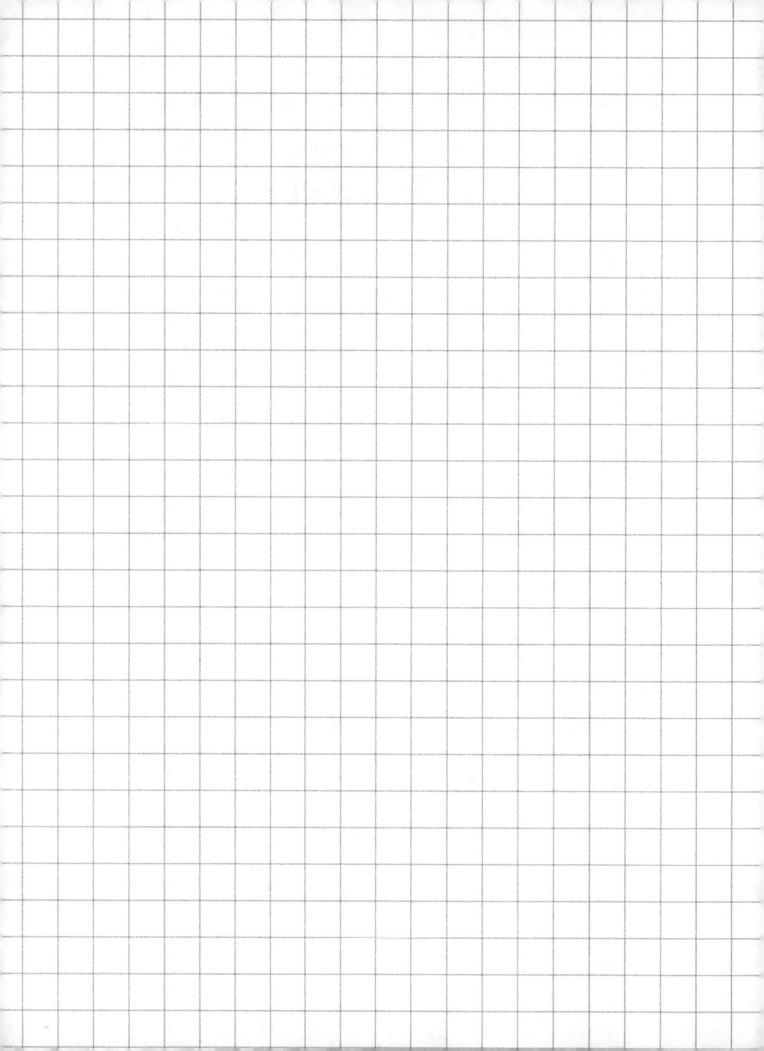

Coordinate Graphing / Draw by Coordinates

To reveal the mystery picture plot and connect the dots with coordinates:
(6, 10), (6, 13), (9, 13), (9, 4), (11, 4), (11, 13), (14, 13), (14, 3), (12, 1),
(8, 1), (6, 3), (6, 5), (7, 6), (8, 8), (8, 9), (7, 10), (6, 10), (5, 9), (4, 10),
(4, 13), (1, 13), (1, 1), (4, 1), (4, 5), (3, 6), (2, 8), (2, 9), (3, 10), (4, 10).

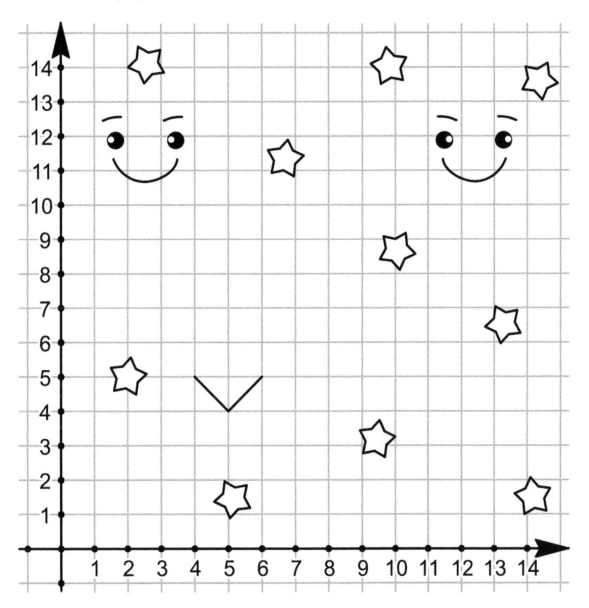

ANSWER:

Coordinate Graphing / Draw by Coordinates

To reveal the mystery picture plot and connect the dots with coordinates:
(9, 6), (11, 4), (13, 6), (14, 8), (14, 9), (13, 10), (12, 10), (11, 9), (10, 10), (9, 10),
(8, 9), (8, 8), (9, 6), (8, 5), (7, 5), (6, 6), (7, 8), (7, 9), (6, 10), (5, 10), (4, 9),
(3, 10), (2, 10), (1, 9), (1, 8), (2, 6), (4, 4), (6, 6) and (2, 6), (1, 5), (3, 5), (3, 2),
(1, 2), (2, 3), (3, 3) and (5, 5), (5, 2), (7, 2), (6, 3), (5, 3) and (10, 5), (10, 2),
(14, 2), (13, 3), (12, 3), (12, 2), (11, 3), (10, 3).

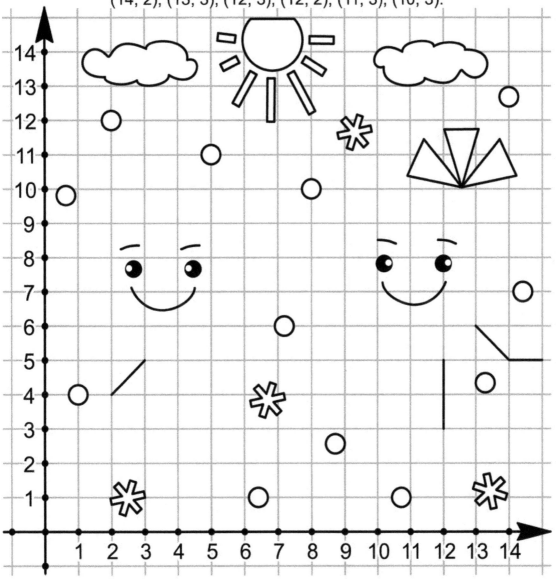

ANSWER:

Coordinate Graphing / Draw by Coordinates

To reveal the mystery picture plot and connect the dots with coordinates:
(2, 6), (3, 6), (3, 10), (2, 10), (3, 12), (4, 12), (4, 6), (5, 6), (5, 12), (8, 12), (8, 6), (9, 6),
(9, 12), (12, 12), (12, 6), (14, 6) and (2, 5), (4, 5), (5, 4), (5, 2), (4, 1), (2, 1), (2, 5)
and (7, 5), (6, 1), (7, 1), (7, 2), (8, 2), (8, 1), (9, 1), (8, 5), (7, 5) and (11, 5), (12, 5),
(11, 3), (11, 1), (10, 1), (10, 3), (9, 5), (10, 5).

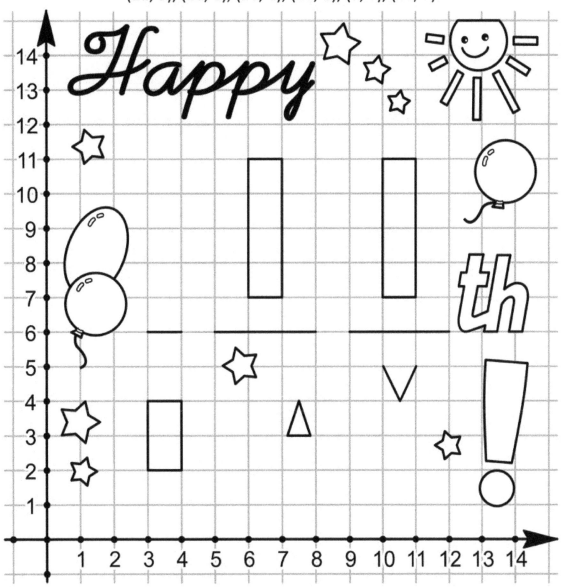

ANSWER:

Coordinate Graphing / Draw by Coordinates

To reveal the mystery picture plot and connect the dots with coordinates:

(7, 14), (7, 13), (6, 13), (8, 7), (10, 13), (9, 13), (9, 14), (14, 14), (14, 13), (13, 13), (9, 1), (7, 1), (3, 13), (2, 13), (2, 14), (7, 14).

ANSWER:

V is for Valentine

Coordinate Graphing / Draw by Coordinates

To reveal the mystery picture plot and connect the dots with coordinates:
(4, 13), (8, 14), (12, 13) and (2, 8), (2, 11), (6, 12), (10, 12), (14, 11), (14, 8)
and (8, 3), (2, 8), (4, 9), (8, 3), (8, 10), (12, 9), (8, 3), (14, 8), (12, 9), (10, 12),
(8, 10), (6, 12), (4, 9), (2, 11), (4, 13), (6, 12), (8, 14), (10, 12), (12, 13),
(14, 11), (12, 9), (14, 8), (8, 3), (12, 9).

ANSWER:

Girls love diamonds

Coordinate Graphing / Draw by Coordinates

To reveal the mystery picture plot and connect the dots with coordinates:
(5, 9), (3, 10), (2, 10), (1, 9), (1, 8), (2, 7), (1, 6), (1, 5), (2, 4), (3, 4), (5, 5), (9, 9),
(11, 10), (12, 10), (13, 9), (13, 8), (12, 7), (13, 6), (13, 5), (12, 4), (11, 4), (9, 5),
(7, 7), (8, 3), (9, 1), (8, 1), (7, 3), (7, 7), (5, 9), (4, 11), (4, 12), (5, 13), (6, 13),
(7, 12), (8, 13), (9, 13), (10, 12), (10, 11), (9, 9).

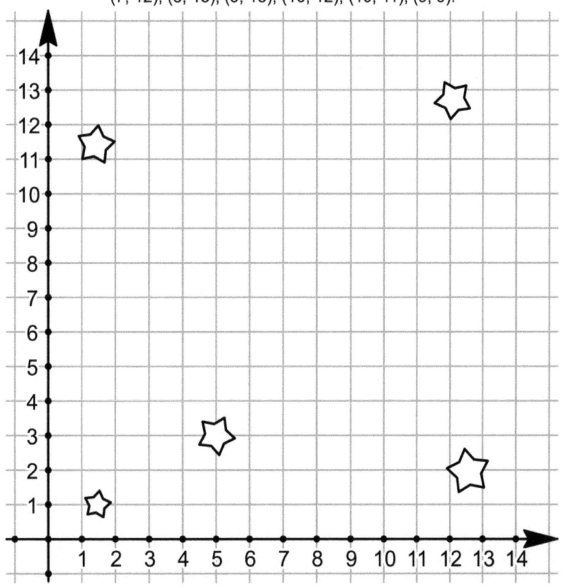

ANSWER:

Coordinate Graphing / Draw by Coordinates

To reveal the mystery picture plot and connect the dots with coordinates:
(8, 4), (10, 6), (10.9), (9, 11), (10, 12), (12, 9), (12, 6), (11, 4), (9, 2),
(5, 2), (3, 4), (2, 6), (2, 9), (4, 12), (5, 11), (4, 9), (4, 6), (6, 4), (8, 4).

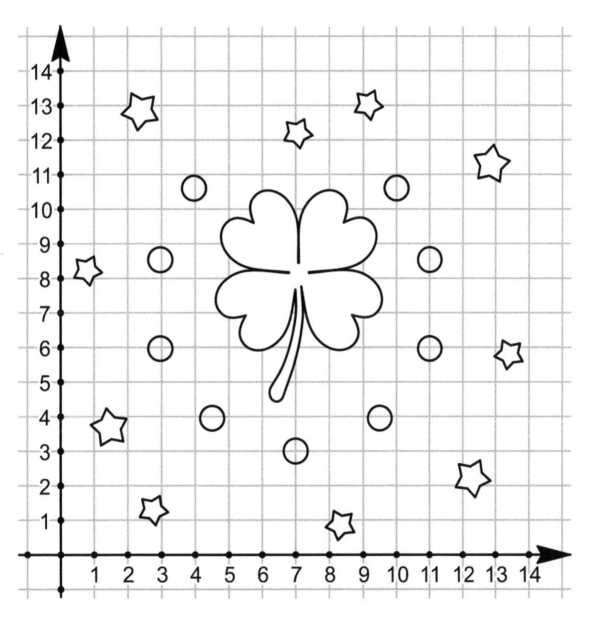

ANSWER:

Coordinate Graphing / Draw by Coordinates

To reveal the mystery picture plot and connect the dots with coordinates:
(4, 6), (1, 7), (6, 6), (8, 6), (13, 7), (10, 6)
and (1, 7), (4, 8), (5, 14), (9, 14), (10, 8), (13, 7).

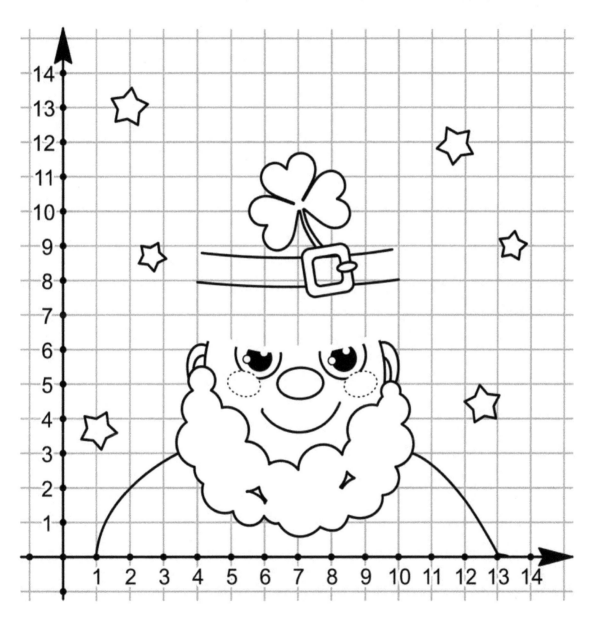

ANSWER:

Coordinate Graphing / Draw by Coordinates

To reveal the mystery picture plot and connect the dots with coordinates:
(6, 13), (6, 1), (3, 1), (3, 10), (1, 9), (1, 10), (4, 13), (6, 13)
and (7, 13), (7, 11), (11, 11), (9, 5), (8, 1), (11, 1), (12, 7), (13, 10),
(14, 12), (14, 13), (7, 13).

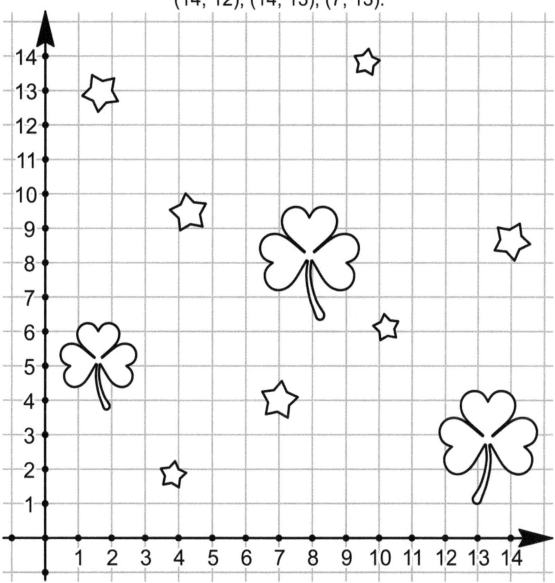

ANSWER:

Coordinate Graphing / Draw by Coordinates

To reveal the mystery picture plot and connect the dots with coordinates:
(10, 8), (11, 7), (12, 5), (11, 3), (10, 2), (10, 1), (9, 2), (6, 2), (5, 1),
(5, 2), (4, 3), (3, 5), (4, 7), (5, 8).

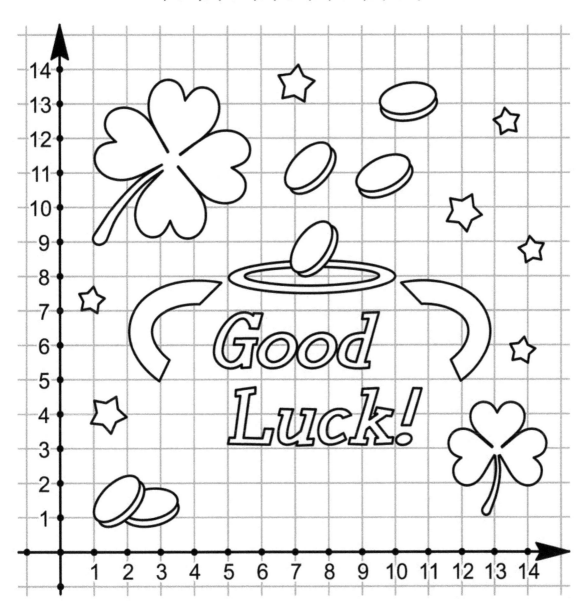

ANSWER:

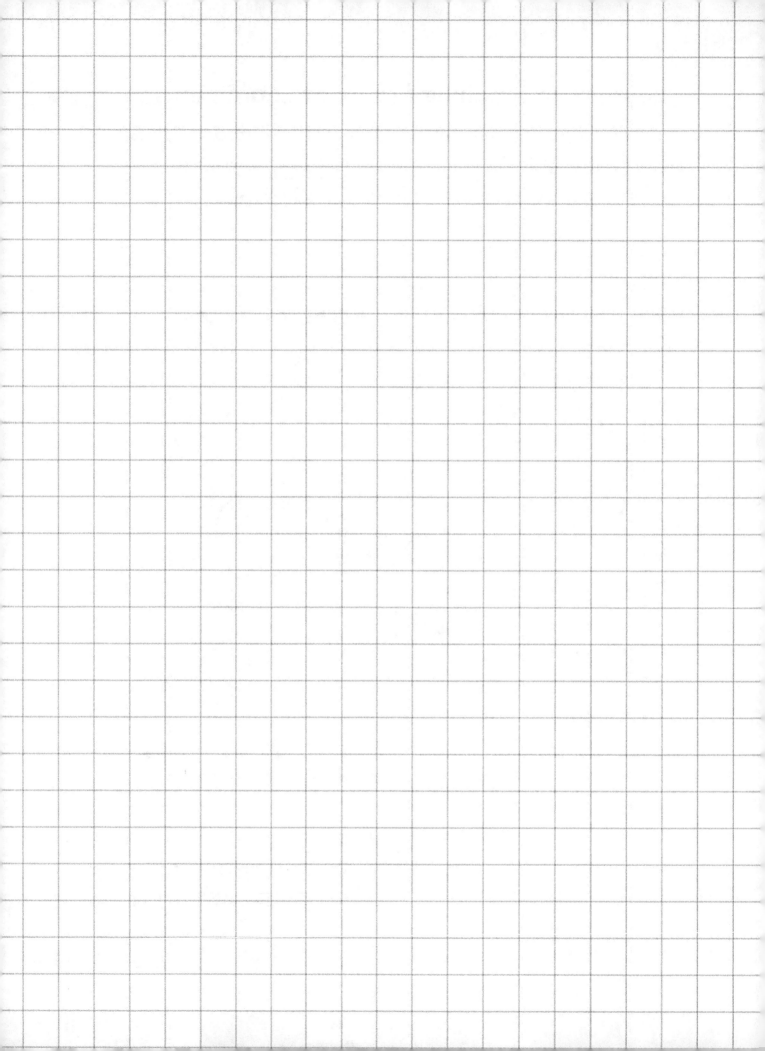

Coordinate Graphing / Draw by Coordinates

To reveal the mystery picture plot and connect the dots with coordinates:
(4, 7), (3, 8), (2, 7), (3, 6), (5, 8), (3, 10), (0, 7), (3, 4), (7, 8), (8, 7), (11, 10), (14, 7), (11, 4), (9, 6), (11, 8), (12, 7), (11, 6), (10, 7) and (6, 7), (10, 3), (7, 0), (4, 3), (6, 5), (8, 3), (7, 2), (6, 3), (7, 4) and (7, 10), (8, 11), (7, 12), (6, 11), (8, 9), (10, 11), (7, 14), (4, 11), (7, 8).

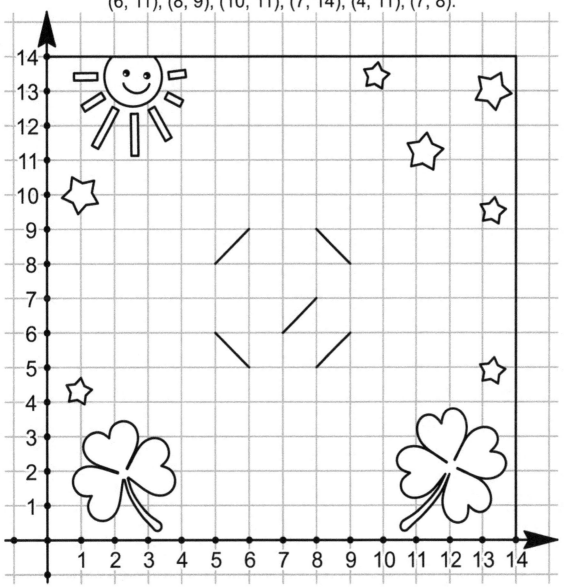

ANSWER:

Coordinate Graphing / Draw by Coordinates

To reveal the mystery picture plot and connect the dots with coordinates:
(6, 11), (8, 9), (9, 7), (9, 4), (8, 2), (6, 1), (4, 1), (2, 2), (1, 4), (1, 7), (2, 9), (4, 11),
(6, 11), (8, 13), (10, 13), (12, 11), (13, 9), (13, 6), (12, 4), (10, 3), (9, 3).

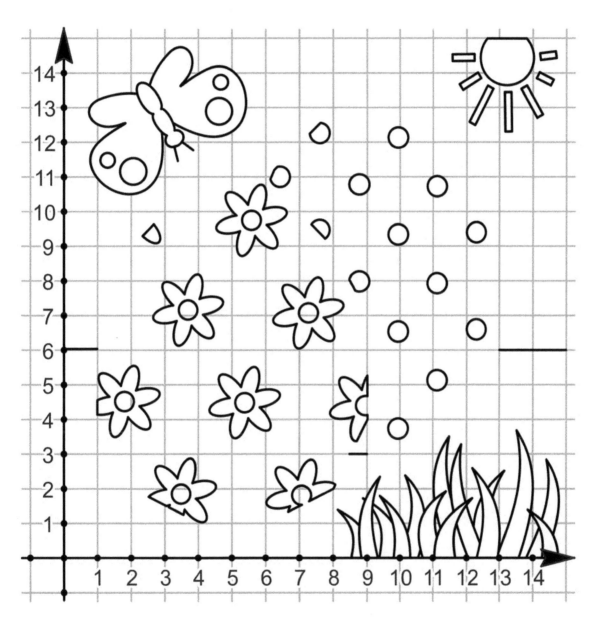

ANSWER:

Coordinate Graphing / Draw by Coordinates

To reveal the mystery picture plot and connect the dots with coordinates:

A: (10, 11), (11, 11), (10, 12), (10, 10), (8, 10), (8, 7), (9, 7), (9, 12), (10, 12). **B:** (4, 5), (1, 4), (1, 2), (4, 1), (11, 1), (14, 2), (14, 4), (11, 5), (10, 5), (11, 4), (12, 4), (12, 3), (3, 3), (3, 4), (4, 4), (4, 6), (6, 8), (7, 8), (8, 10), (10, 10), (11, 9), (11, 8), (10, 7), (10, 5). **C:** (8, 6), (8, 5), (9, 4), (10, 4), (10, 3). **D:** (5, 6), (6, 6), (7, 5), (7, 4), (8, 4), (8, 3).

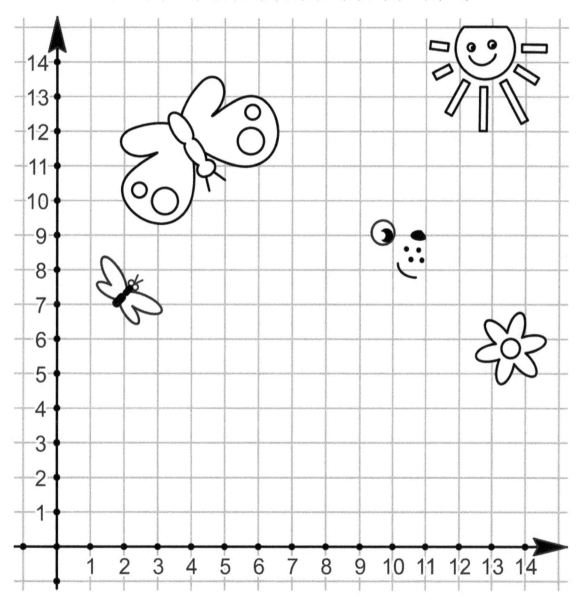

ANSWER:

Coordinate Graphing / Draw by Coordinates

To reveal the mystery picture plot and connect the dots with coordinates:

A: (11, 11), (12, 10), (13, 7), (12, 3). **B:** (13, 7), (9, 6), (6, 6), (2, 7), (3, 3), (6, 2), (9, 2). **C:** (2, 7), (3, 10), (5, 12), (7, 13), (8, 13), (10, 12).

ANSWER:

Coordinate Graphing / Draw by Coordinates

To reveal the mystery picture plot and connect the dots with coordinates:
(12, 5), (11, 3), (9, 2), (7, 2), (5, 3), (4, 5), (4, 8), (5, 10), (7, 12), (9, 12), (11, 10), (12, 8), (12, 5).

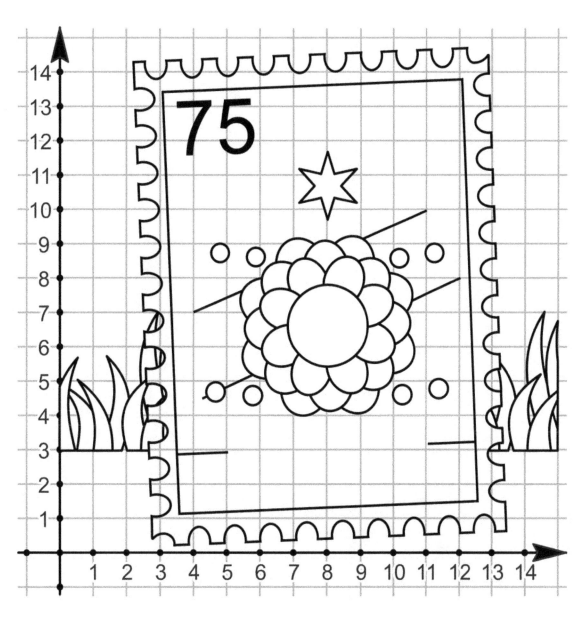

ANSWER:

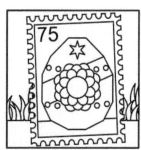

Coordinate Graphing / Draw by Coordinates

To reveal the mystery picture plot and connect the dots with coordinates:

A: (5, 3), (5, 2), (6, 2), (6, 7), (5, 7), (4, 5), (3, 2), (3, 3), (2, 3), (2, 4), (3, 4), (3, 5), (2, 5), (2, 6), (3, 6), (3, 7), (1, 7), (1, 2), (4, 2). **B:** (6, 3), (7, 3), (7, 2), (6, 2), (6, 1), (8, 1), (8, 6), (7, 6), (7, 7), (10, 7), (10, 6), (11, 6), (11, 7), (13, 7), (14, 6), (14, 5), (13, 4), (14, 2), (13, 2), (12, 4), (12, 2), (10, 2), (10, 3), (11, 3), (11, 1), (9, 1), (9, 6), (10, 6).

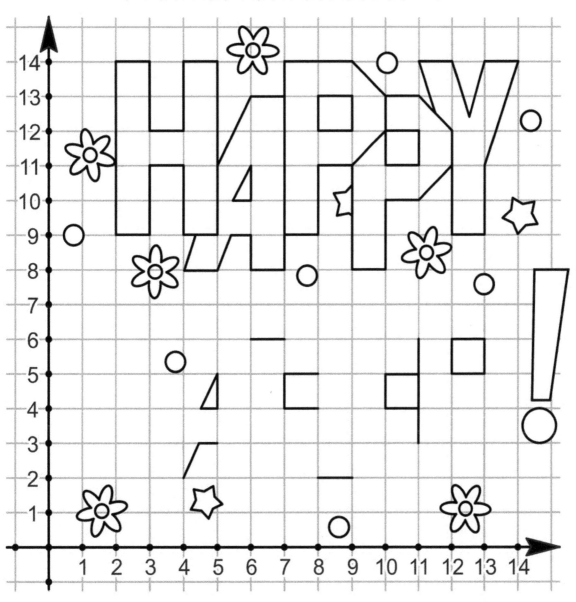

ANSWER:

CPSIA information can be obtained
at www.ICGtesting.com
Printed in the USA
BVHW052307011221
622871BV00011B/253